Soul Freedom, Sacred Aliveness

An Extraordinary Guide to Coming Unconditionally Alive

Mark Schoofs

ISBN: 978-0-9821767-0-2

Library of Congress Control Number: 2009908407

Design by Mark Schoofs, Carolyn Hedger and Karin Kinsey

SoulWorks Publishing, St. Petersburg, FL 33704

Printed in the USA

2nd Edition

Dedication

This book is dedicated with all my love to all those students and clients who have, each in their own way, contributed their consciousness and their love to my journey of awakening. No words could possibly convey the gratitude and honor I feel for having been able to work with them and serve them.

Soul Freedom, Sacred Aliveness

Introduction 7

1. Radical Aliveness 13

2. Letting Go 15

3. The Conditioned Mind 19

4. Life Itself Is the Answer 25

5. Easy Does It—Or Does It? 31

6. Tuning in to Sacred Aliveness 37

7. Higher Mind 49

8. Soul Mission 61

9. Staying True to Love 71

10. Blessing, Gratitude and the Rhythm of
    Awareness and Healing 93

11. The Ascendancy of the Sacred Feminine 111

12. Grounding and Presence 121

13. Evolution and the Paradigm Shift 151

14. Incarnating the Living Spirit 157

15. Taking the Leap—Transcending the
    Conditional Self 167

16. Conscious Soul Freedom 185

17. Co-Creating a Sacred World 205

    CDs by Mark Schoofs 224

Introduction

In the spring of 1988 I found myself feeling deeply and mysteriously restless. At the time I lived in my native state of Iowa. I had a very good life there, with a great place to live in the country surrounded by nature, an exciting relationship with a wonderful partner, and a thriving community life with many friends who, like me, were keenly involved in impassioned personal growth and metaphysical activities of many kinds. Yet I felt strangely restless. I felt that, somehow, powerful winds of change were gathering force in my life.

The feelings grew stronger and stronger. I saw the signs of change showing up first in my relationship. My partner and I started noticing that we weren't quite there for each other like we used to be, and that this was okay, and that a time of new freedom was beginning for each of us. Next, an old friend saw my restlessness and decided to nudge me along. He gifted me with a substantial sum of cash with the message *Mark, it's time for you to expand your horizons* written all over the gift. The winds of change were building force and starting to take over. A friend came forward asking if he could buy one of the two vehicles I owned—fine, I handed him the keys. My restlessness felt so heightened by then that I don't think I could have resisted it, and by summer I was letting go of my life as I had known it. I held a big moving sale. Some friends staged a farewell party. I threw what was leftover from the sale into my old Dodge van, and drove west.

I didn't know where I would wind up. I didn't have a clue about how I would make a living. But I was moving on, as I felt I had to.

I spent a couple of weeks in Colorado, and marked my fortieth birthday there. Some folks I met at Copper Mountain had good things to say about Eugene, Oregon. I liked the gut feeling I got about Eugene and decided to go there.

What a uniquely heartening, magical city! It was easy to see why folks grow fond of Eugene. I found a nice apartment and settled in. Within a short while I found myself calling a spiritual teacher I had met in Iowa when she was teaching there. She gave scintillating workshops, and I remembered that she actually lived in northern California. "Would you like to come up to Eugene and give a workshop here?" I asked her. I was eager to have a weekend of spiritual invigoration, and to share it with new friends in my new town. She agreed to dates. I agreed to organize it.

 While she was spending time with me in Eugene, after the workshop, she remarked to me, "You know, Mark, you didn't really need to invite me to give this workshop. You could give it yourself."

I had not seen *that* coming.

But I didn't block it. I made up a sample flyer, just to see what would happen.

Soon I was being invited to give workshops in various places around Oregon. And from the very first workshop, held in a quaint, rustic yurt in the woods near Bandon, Oregon, I knew that I had discovered my true life work and my true life passion. Now I wasn't restless anymore. Now I was keen on exploring my calling. It seemed I had a natural gift for facilitating spiritual awakening.

Before long I was invited to teach at Mt. Shasta, California, a legendary "power spot" or energy vortex fifty miles south of the Oregon border. I had heard about the power of Mt. Shasta. But experiencing the energies of the area, first-hand, was spiritually galvanizing in a way that I simply could not have anticipated. Mt. Shasta, I discovered, is the type of place where consciousness can tune in very readily to the living planes of energy within things, and where the sacred Source, the indwelling infinite Spirit, comes so alive in consciousness that one feels awash in universal sacred aliveness.

It was only a matter of time before I gravitated to Mt. Shasta and left my Eugene days behind. I spent three years based at Mt. Shasta. Those years were like an intensive apprenticeship in energy sensitivity, heightened awareness, energy healing, and soul fitness. I was giving workshops, on a relatively small scale, around northern California and parts of Oregon. Meanwhile every day at Mt. Shasta, when I wasn't traveling, was like a *personal* workshop between me and Spirit. It felt like everything inside me that resisted the sacred aliveness was being brought to the surface to see if I could clear it. This was an arduous time for me. I had some help from others along the way, but mostly my path was one of inner learning and inner apprenticeship with Spirit. I learned in many ways to track my inner awareness habits and to develop my spiritual fitness skills.

I learned, most of all, that beyond all the metaphysical insights and all the healing techniques and skills, it is the well tested purity, fidelity, and resourcefulness of spiritual love, abiding deep within, that can illumine and transform all.

I have been teaching that and practicing that ever since.

At some point in the early 1990s I was "discovered" more widely as a teacher and a healer and started traveling nationwide, while continuing to lead groups on Mt. Shasta every summer. I've been told that my gift is to "jump start" people into more conscious expression of their own spiritual presence, their own divine soul presence. For individuals and for groups, I seem to able to tune in to the next steps of insight, blessing, healing, and awakening that are ripening for them on higher planes, and to facilitate the timely and appropriate movement of these steps of growth into their conscious experience.

This can take any form. I never plan or impose. For me, the work is always about tuning my awareness to the currents of living wisdom in the One Mind or Higher Mind, and letting this flow into appropriate expression. I will always remember one day in 1991 when I was working at a booth at the Whole Life Expo in San Francisco. I had a little sign posted, saying I was giving readings and healings. A woman approached the booth and asked, "If I get a session with you, what will you do?"

I must have been feeling especially spontaneous and honest at the moment, so I said, "I don't know."

"Good!" she said. "I'll take one."

And I realized how this made perfect sense. She had just validated my instincts, my instincts to always keep my work as spontaneous and Spirit-based as possible.

I'm a big believer in spontaneous, first-hand experience. That's why I always say, to workshop groups as well as to individual clients, "I'm just giving words to what there's energy for, right here right now. Hopefully the words are helping—the words arise from the energy and serve the energy—but know that, beyond the words, the energy is real. *Go with the energy. Go with the experience.*"

My wish is that this book prove deeply experiential in the reading. It has certainly proved deeply experiential in the writing. And for me, the experience keeps growing and evolving. The book is complete, but the experience will always keep growing.

✧   ✧   ✧

This book springs from a very simple perspective on spiritual awakening: human consciousness is evolving to a threshold in which we grasp, with every bit of our being, that—

✧ Aliveness is sacred, universal, and whole.

✧ We are meant to *come alive,* and to come alive all the way, to come alive *unconditionally.*

✧ The only way to come alive unconditionally is to transcend our limited, conditional consciousness and let the infinite Spirit, the sacred Source of life, live fully in us, as us.

Once we reach this threshold of total lucid insight that we can come alive unconditionally by simply letting Spirit live in us, as us, then we see that—

✧ We are already free to move through the threshold.

In fact *we have always been free* to move through this threshold! That is the extraordinary thing about it. We are already free to be unconditionally alive in the sacred aliveness of the One, of the living Spirit.

This pure and utter freedom of the soul is so pivotal to our awakening, as it opens us into truly unconditional realms of spiritual happiness, power, wisdom, and most of all love.

I call this heightened perspective *Soul Freedom, Sacred Aliveness.*

The vision of *Soul Freedom, Sacred Aliveness* has become the central, organizing vision around which everything I have come to understand about spiritual awakening revolves. Chapter 4 recounts some of the story of how this perspective grew and matured for me, in my life. My wish for you, as you spend time with this book, is that each chapter carry you further into the vision as it is meant to awaken and mature for you.

The chapters build on each other sequentially, and I do recommend reading the book sequentially, at least the first time through. Chapter 4 and for that matter the first five chapters are all brief and foundational—they are meant to give you a "springboard" into what follows.

Truth is a living thing, and we can never capture it fully in words or direct it fully in words. But each of us can let the living truth find expression in us, when we "go with the energy" as we are feeling it, and "go with the experience" as we are feeling it. So go with your own ripening experience, especially in the chapters containing indented sections of guided experience. These sections are meant to awaken new pathways of ever more resonant vision and living truth in your awareness.

Truth lives and inheres in the ongoing activity of the infinite Spirit. Spirit is always actively generating fresh currents of energy to bless and support our individual lives and our personal awakening. This activity of the infinite Spirit is a "given." What is variable is how well we bond to the activity of the infinite, so that we can work with it, consciously. If there is a way to bond fully and utterly to the blessings of Spirit, I believe that way is, simply, love. It's built into how the Universe works: when we are centered in the purity of our love, we bond directly into the ongoing activity of Spirit and we can work with Spirit, consciously, to awaken into unconditional aliveness.

The threshold of awakening is always beckoning us. The conscious experience of *Soul Freedom, Sacred Aliveness* is always immanent, in every moment. I have tried to hone this book to just that, to the luminous reality that draws us all to live soulfully and passionately, moment by moment, in the sacred aliveness of the infinite Spirit.

Mark Schoofs

Chapter 1

Radical Aliveness

I have always resonated deeply to the idea that, if you had to say what the opposite of life is, you would be on the wrong track if you said the answer is death. In fact, any answer at all would take you off track. You can check this with your inner wisdom. All your inner wisdom knows is life. This is the resonant truth. Life is all there is.

If at all there are opposites, the opposites are, simply—

✧ Allowing life, versus
✧ Resisting life.

In either case, allowing or resisting, life is the one reality.

Life is a radical subject.

Chapter 2

Letting Go

Spiritual awakening begins when we slip beyond the constraints of normal consciousness. The slightest shift in this direction can refresh our inner being and stir the inner wisdom of life within us.

This inner wisdom is the part of us that knows how to—

✧ Allow life, and
✧ Let go of whatever resists life.

Easy Does It

Letting go is meant to be very easy. The living wisdom within us already knows how to do it. In fact if we know anything at all, we know how to let go. If letting go was difficult, would we want to call it letting go? Probably not.

We have an innate instinct to let go of whatever resists or restricts life. Judgment, hurt, worry, doubt, tension, sadness, etc.—these things restrict the life-force within us and invite our inner wisdom to transform and transcend them, to heal them and let them go, so that our awareness can freely commune in its most natural state, the authentic state of sacred aliveness.

This is what our inner wisdom knows—*unconditional, unlimited sacred aliveness.*

Another way to say this is that our inner wisdom, as wisdom, participates in universal truth, and the truth is that our life-force is sourced from the infinite Spirit as our share in the sacred aliveness of the infinite.

Each part of an infinite whole is, itself, infinite. And so our own life-force, our personal experience of aliveness, is, when we penetrate to its essence, unlimited.

Meanwhile, of course, our conditioned mind feels it's on solid ground believing that things like limitedness, pain, loss, and death define our reality. That's okay, actually—it just tells us that the conditioned mind and the inner wisdom are working on different levels. So we might think of *letting go* as an *invitation to let ourselves move to another level.* Letting go is an invitation to let ourselves move to a level where we can draw on the natural instincts of our indwelling living wisdom.

This movement, this vibrational shift in our awareness, is a first step on the path of spiritual awakening. It takes us just beyond the constraints of normal consciousness.

Wisdom Is Alive

This first step is perhaps the only step we really need to take, because it gives the living wisdom a chance to express and flow. The point is that this wisdom is *living.* It is endowed with divine life-force, it *is* divine life-force. It knows what to do. It knows how to evolve our minds and hearts, taking us ultimately into conscious oneness with the Source of life.

Living wisdom is not something we work on. Wisdom is abiding truth.

When we "work on ourselves," when we work on self-improvement practices, etc., we may participate in the abiding truth of life, or we may not—but in either case the truth abides and lives within us. The key is to be consciously attuned to the living truth. Then it becomes a direct vibrational experience that refreshes, inspires, and evolves our awareness.

Then the living truth becomes our *personal* truth.

The first step is letting go.

Letting go reminds our personal awareness that its job is to participate in something bigger than itself.

Letting go reminds our personal awareness that its job is to participate in something that is unconditional and unlimited.

Chapter 3

The Conditioned Mind

Imagine you are perched in a hot air balloon's basket. The balloon above you swells with hot air, the sky is a glorious blue, the breeze is blowing strong and fresh.

You have a look around you—and, to your astonishment, you're stuck on the ground, going nowhere! As you get your bearings you see what the problem is—the basket is full of heavy old stuff, trunks and satchels and suitcases of it, and it's all your personal stuff, your *baggage.* And it's weighing you down.

So keen as you were, or thought you were, on soaring happily into the heavens, now you've got to bend down and deal with your personal stuff. This is a key moment. Will you follow your true instinct and toss all that baggage, or will you find, as you bend over it, that you can't really let go of it, that you're drawn into it, that you want to spend time with your things, handling them, perhaps even cherishing them, holding onto them?

What will you do?

What would happen if we could toss all our accumulated stuff out of the way and get on with the higher instincts of our life? It's obvious, we would soar into heightened states of awareness and aliveness.

Why do we normally act like we have not figured this out?

Because we have not been willing to trust that moving into heightened states really will make us happy.

Why has our trust been lacking?

Because we are attached, even addicted, whether we know it or not, to the wrong kind of happiness.

Conditional Happiness

In the hot air balloon metaphor, the baggage represents *all our conditioned, personal agendas and beliefs about what makes us happy.* We tend to set conditions for being happy. "I'll be happy if this happens" or "I'll be happy if that doesn't happen," etc. It would probably take the average person just a few moments of reflection to come up with a whole list of ways in which they tell themselves they will be happy if and when certain conditions come together just right, from relatively trivial things like "I'll be happy when 5 o'clock comes and I can leave work for the day, but only if I'm not too tired by then," to major agendas like "I'll be happy when I find true love," or "I'll be happy when the divorce is final." The conditions for happiness are forever changing while, all along, the direct and full *experience* of happiness, *in the moment,* tends to elude us.

The wounded psyche skates and maneuvers on the surface of the problem as it keeps looking for ways to "set things right." Meanwhile the whole perception that things need to be "set right" is driven by inner layers of feeling that go largely unreckoned and unresolved.

These layered feelings include—

✧ All our *judgments* of the people and circumstances we feel are unacceptable or threatening.

✧ All the *anger and hurt* beneath the judgment.

✧ All the *disappointment* and *sadness* beneath the hurt.

✧ All the *needing* and *yearning for love and approval and success* beneath the sadness.

✧ All the *personal inadequacy feelings* beneath the yearning for love and approval and success.

✧ All the *fear and weakness* beneath the personal inadequacy feelings.

Ultimately, beneath the fear and weakness, it always comes down to—

✧ The *core belief that we are separate and on our own in the universe.*

Separation Wounding

This core wound, this belief in separation and aloneness, can be found within all our conditional agendas for happiness, with corresponding layers of unresolved feeling and unresolved desire. It's our way of nursing the feeling that we don't know for sure, we can't trust for certain, that Spirit is really there for us, or that the spiritual connection can really take care of us.

Investment

And so we take it upon ourselves to try to take care of ourselves—and as soon as this starts, the phenomenon of *investment* begins.

When we examine our baggage we see that it is not just some kind of amorphous "stuff" that we carry around. We see that it is invested with tremendous amounts of our own energy. We have literally flowed our life-force through our issues and dramas, investing them with a kind of vital importance and resonance.

Desire energy is power. When we invest our desire for happiness in conditional agendas and beliefs, we *give our power* to these agendas and beliefs.

The Conditioned Mind

To the mind that knows it has invested so much of itself in the conditional approach to happiness, abandoning its efforts seems impossible. We could call this mind the *conditioned mind.* And it is true that the conditioned mind, left to itself, cannot find a way to abandon its cherished efforts. The conditioned mind really does believe that, as its conditions are met, happiness ensues—and so the conditioned mind stays entrained in its own program.

This can leave us feeling pretty earthbound, both metaphysically speaking and, in the metaphor of the hot air balloon, literally. The conditioned mind behaves in ways that are patently earthbound.

The conditioned mind functions
according to the laws of third-dimensional
or "earth-plane" existence,
without a sense of higher laws.

When it comes to seeking happiness, the conditioned mind is bound by the third-dimensional law of cause and effect: "If only I could get such and such conditions met, *then* I would be happy." Built into this mind-set is the principle of—

✧ Linear time ("If only...*then*...")

and the related principles of—

✧ Finite time ("If I don't get my conditions met, I'll run out of time"); and
✧ Finite resources ("If I don't get what I want, someone else will get to be happy instead of me, because there's not enough for everyone.")

In a world of such drastic limitation, the conditioned mind is chronically tense and self-involved. And the more self-involved it gets, the less capable it is of being truly refreshed. Self-involved systems are like that. The conditioned mind may feel better when it succeeds in getting what it wants, it may in fact feel elated—but even this success phase, like every other phase of conditional experience, is, by definition, *conditional.* The success could be lost. The happiness could fade. *No conditions are permanent.*

The Essential Quandary:

Seeking Happiness Blocks Happiness

Something has to give here. The conditional approach to happiness has got to be let go of. But what is it going to take to really release it?

The hot air balloon metaphor makes it obvious that we've got to learn to release—however the process of doing so may not be so simple. When I lead groups in the hot air balloon visualization, participants sometimes discover that their baggage feels like it has been there so long that it has become ingrown, part of the balloon itself. It is as if their baggage is so invested with life-force that it has grown living roots that entangle and enmesh themselves in the very fabric and weave of the basket. This represents how our personal identity itself, the whole aspiring enterprise of consciousness that we call self, can feel chronically enmeshed in the conditional search for happiness.

Again, something has to give. We cannot expect the conditioned mind to provide the solution. We are already pushing the mind to its rational limit by recognizing the essential quandary as it is—that is, by recognizing that *seeking happiness has been blocking happiness.* This is more than the conditioned mind can reconcile.

The solution will need to be radical.

Chapter 4

Life Itself Is the Answer

Life carries us forward. Life knows what it's doing. If we are staying truly present to what life is, we come around to seeing, with compelling clarity, that—

  ✧ Life is all there is. We can allow life or resist life,
      but life is all there is.
  ✧ Life is evolving.
  ✧ Life is inviting us, in every way it can, to *let go* of our
      resistance, *let go* of our investment in the conditional
      approach to happiness, and allow ourselves to really
      come alive, without conditions—radically alive,
      unconditionally alive.

An Unconditional State of Being Alive

What happens when we finally transcend the conditional approach to happiness and move into an unconditional, radical state of aliveness?

I got my answer, firsthand, in September of 1998. The weave of my personal life had become seriously frayed that year by a series of gut-wrenching life-changes. The preceding twelve months had featured a very painful relationship break-up; a relocation move to northern California only to see the late autumn turn into an El Niño winter of record-setting rainfall, flooding, and mudslides; an unprecedented flu season that turned my immune system into a viral free-for-all; and an exploratory move to Maui that just didn't seem meant to work out happily either and was abruptly ended by the unexpected death of my mother. Each life-change had taken me deeper into personal crisis feelings. The upside was that, by then, I was developing a fairly functional sense of how soul perspective is supposed to work in life—that we're here on a soul mission to demonstrate how inner divine love can transform all experience into a joyous, unconditional state of peace—and I knew I was being called upon to practice this. So I was focusing ever more intensely on freeing myself of the turbulent effects of outer circumstances by learning to live in the inner realm of soul. The more I let go of conditioned mind investment in having my life "work out" the way I thought I wanted it to, the more my awareness was shifting toward a state of free and unconditional aliveness.

By September of '98 the turbulent circumstances were reaching a peak. My conditioned mind and its abc's for finding happiness—its agendas, beliefs, and conditions for "setting things right"—were feeling painfully unfit.

I didn't know what to do.

I thought of Mt. Shasta, California, where many of the most spiritually formative experiences of my life have taken place, and I decided to go there for a week of retreat. I knew that the spiritual energies of the Mt. Shasta area create a powerful vortex for change and transformation. That was what I needed.

Vortex

I took a room at a little retreat house with a view of the mountain. I was the only one there, the summer season was over, a fall chill was in the air.

I lay in my room, rested in my soul, and let go.

It was then that the vortex opened up to me. The whole area came alive to my inner vision with the most profound energy currents I had ever felt, currents of pure, ecstatic life-force. Everything was dancing in this pure ecstatic aliveness and as this sacred aliveness swirled through me and commingled with my awareness I was swept into a heightened state of soul arousal.

I spent the next several days awash in this. All my senses, all my feelings, all my knowing were cleansed and lifted in the universal sacred aliveness. I saw that we are meant to live in a state of utter and complete soul grace. I saw that each of us, as souls made whole by our journey, is meant to stand in a state of utter and complete soul freedom. That from the perspective of the infinite living Spirit there is actually nothing to let go of anyhow, that *we are already free,* if we but allow our freedom and trust it and live it.

In the eyes of Spirit we are innately and purely and forever free, if we but relax into our freedom and let be what it must be—*unconditional.*

Letting It Be Unconditional

This is the state of grace—the unconditional freedom of the soul to live in the universal currents of pure, ecstatic sacred aliveness.

I saw that, in this state, we are free to be happy—unconditionally.

I saw that we are free to love—unconditionally.

I saw that we are free to have our highest good—unconditionally. We are free to live consciously in our divinely endowed state of inner good—which is beyond conditions—and so to attract from the world around us the purest possible reflections of our good.

Most of all, I saw that we are free to *be alive*—unconditionally.

And I saw that there is only one way to be alive unconditionally—

We come alive unconditionally
when we allow the universal sacred aliveness,
the pure, ecstatic life-force
that springs from the infinite Spirit and animates all things,
to live consciously in us as our life-force,
as our true nature.

Unconditional Aliveness

Is Naturally Whole

When we come unconditionally alive in this way we experience a natural state of wholeness. We directly experience life as whole. We know beyond doubt that we are an integral part of the sacred wholeness of life and that, like any part, we *participate* in the wholeness. We directly feel, for example, how the well being of the whole affects our personal well being, and vice versa. We become keenly conscious of how interconnected all of life is. We know beyond doubt that we are not separate and on our own.

An Unconditional State of Being Happy

When we come unconditionally alive, *then* we can experience unconditional happiness. This is because the nature of pure aliveness is
joy. This joy is unconditional, based on nothing *about* our life. Unconditional happiness is grounded utterly in pure aliveness itself. It
is happiness on the level of Spirit. It is the authentic experience of the
living Spirit. And as such it is absolute. Timeless. Perfect.[1]

And so we realize that happiness is our nature—not our goal.

We come to see that we cannot need what we already are.

And we realize that we never need to renew our true happiness,
though we may need to renew our authentic experience of the living
Spirit. We may need to transcend agendas, beliefs, and conditions and
come alive, once again, in the experience of Spirit living in us, as us.

Soul Arousal

This vision, as it awakened in me, felt much more real and substantial than anything else that was going on in my life—and truly it was.
It was a knowingness so profound that, as I learned to center in it,
my whole way of being present in the world was fundamentally and
radically renewed. My whole sense of my life path began to feel on
course in a deeper and more soulfully conscious way. The vision of
Soul Freedom, Sacred Aliveness was imprinted at the core of me.

It is what I now carry—even as it carries me. The vision of totally free, soul conscious, unconditionally joyous aliveness defines
and sustains all of my work. It fills me with inexpressible feelings of
peace, inspiration, and ultimate completion.

---

1 This is the *ananda*, or bliss, as it is known in classical India.

✧　　　✧　　　✧

Imagine the breezes are freshening with new life and the sky is becoming luminous with the play of an ambient, higher-dimensional light. Feel how, deep inside of you, as well, there is a stirring of new aliveness. What you are feeling now is more than the simple calling to soar into this magnificent realm of freedom and light. What you are feeling now is an opening of your very being. And as you open, the freedom and light are not just beckoning you— they are *becoming* you.

As you open, you are not just drawn to the higher reality. You *belong* there, *already,* for it has been your higher truth all along.

You feel a new lightness of being as you look at the baggage onboard your hot air balloon, and at the earth-bound restraint your balloon has been held in. Will it take courage? conviction? faith? to toss the baggage and be free? If it takes courage you have it. If it takes conviction you have it. If it takes faith you have it. What you are feeling, in the lightness of your being, is not particularly courage, conviction, or faith—but simply havingness. Today you are learning that your true, inner being subsumes all having and all good. That whatever is truly good for you, you have.

There is no limited, conditioned self to be enmeshed in the having. There is only this fully free, fully enfranchised, true Self. The real You. The divine Soul.

You feel alive and free as you bend over the baggage in your hot air balloon basket. It looks so out of place now. So you toss it overboard.

And you soar.

Chapter 5

Easy Does It—Or Does It?

Life must evolve. Life *must* evolve—we can count on it that life will seek out ways to press the issue. We can count on it that life will seek out ways to invite us to let go of our resistance, let go of our conditional approach to happiness, and allow ourselves to come radically, unconditionally alive.

There is no particular reason why these invitations need to show up in our lives in the form of challenge or crisis, as they did for me in 1998. Yet they often do show up that way. Why? Are we poor learners? Do we need the stakes to go way high before we can learn to let go of the limited mind and the conditional approach to happiness? Is it really true, as we affirmed in Chapter 2, that letting go is meant to be exquisitely easy, a natural outflowing of the inner wisdom of life? And if so, why is it so complicated at times, why does it get so painfully difficult, to simply let go, to genuinely let go and let ourselves live freely in our most natural state, the state of unconditional sacred aliveness?

This whole pattern of vacillation, this deep, archetypal current of uncertainty and ambivalence, recapitulates, in effect, the very journey of the soul.

The Journey of the Soul

The pattern goes like this—

- ✧ As divinely endowed souls, we start our journey in a state of innocence and grace, a natural state of soul freedom and sacred aliveness.
- ✧ Then we complicate things with layers of separation wounding and with limiting conditions, agendas, and beliefs about whether we're still okay.
- ✧ Then we rediscover our innocence and grace at a higher turn of the spiral where our consciousness, more tuned and more fit from what it has been through, can *own* its natural state of soul freedom and sacred aliveness with new maturity, command, and conscious wholeness.

So to the evolving soul, taking its turns on the spiral of life, the knack of letting go and allowing the natural state of freedom can be, by turns, *both* exquisitely easy *and* painfully difficult.

This state of affairs sets up in consciousness a tension that is inherently dynamic and creative. As the tension grows, issues and uncertainties grow too. Is it really necessary to go through these arduous stages of innocence and loss, one following the other? Will the spiral ever end? Or will it go on and on like a dance of perfectly matched polar opposites? Where is the fulfillment? Are we meant to see the dance itself as fulfilling? And is it? To the soul on its journey, in the midst of it all, these are open questions, with immense consequences and, often, a dizzying spin of implications, subquestions and uncertainties.

This is good. The mounting tension is inherently creative.

The tension compels us to go deeply within and draw near, if we can, to the very foundational level of soul consciousness.

Foundations

At this level, the infinite Beingness of Spirit sets in motion the stream of miracles that leads to the manifest worlds, soul consciousness, and individual life. What is important to understand is that, as soul consciousness and individual life begin to arise, *divine will,* timeless, whole and perfect unto itself, *shares its creative nature with us.* This means that we are invited to share in the creativity of Spirit, that—

We are beckoned to explore
what can be co-created
out of the infinite divine potentials of life.

As this dance of co-creation unfolds, we see that—

✧ Our Source, pure aliveness, the essence or Beingness of Spirit, is unconditionally sacred and whole, vast, oceanic.

✧ This pure aliveness is birthing our individual life into form, much as the ocean rises in waves.

✧ Our individual life is simply the play and interplay of the infinite divine potentials of pure aliveness, much like the play of waves on the surface of the ocean.

✧ Our individual life is learning to draw on the power of its Source, to draw freely and powerfully, so that we can swell and rise in our own unique way, at times arduous, at times inspired, to display the full beauty and potency and utter sacredness of our infinite Source, pure aliveness.

As this perspective holds true in us we come to see, with ever more lucid soul freedom, that—

Our life is simply about the play and interplay
of creative potentials.

In this perspective, each of us, as a divine soul, is lovingly birthed into an arena of infinite creative potentials, each of us freely explores, and each of us ultimately learns.

What We Are Learning

We are learning that Yes, we *can* live by divine principle, we *can* live in a natural state of innocence and grace, of authentic soul freedom and sacred aliveness. We are learning that the key element is simply conscious choice, or will.

The divine will of Spirit is already in place. Divine will, as we said earlier, is timeless and perfect. The infinite Spirit is eternally sponsoring our individual lives to unfold in their most natural state.

But what about the dance of co-creation? What about the bonding of the infinite and the individual, of the divine will and the personal will?

Our personal will may not be so impeccably in place. (We will be looking at this very carefully in Chapter 15.) Our personal will gets engorged with personal choices. Every little flicker of doubt about whether the infinite Spirit is really there for us ("Will trying to align myself to the unseen Spirit really take care of my needs?"); every little flicker of separation anxiety ("I'd better take it upon myself to get what happiness I can on my own, else I won't be happy,") and separation wounding ("I feel so inadequate," or "I feel upset with so-and-so because they don't give me what I want"); every little tweak of the conditioned mind ("I think I may need *this* to make me happy," or "I think I'm not going to be okay until I get *that*,")—all this engorges our personal will with new choices.

Often, these choices confound our essential work, the work of bonding our personal will to the divine will of the infinite Spirit.

The Dance Gets Complicated, But the Dance Is Simple

Happily, there is a destined outcome: because divine will is eternally perfect, it shall prevail. But just how long it's going to take to reach this outcome—that is a totally open question. It may take a very long time. As long as our personal will is invited to participate in the co-creative dance of individual life and evolution, we'll always find that variability, uncertainty, and personal choice are in the equation. The dance is *meant* to be simple. But when our personal will is not very well bonded to Spirit, the dance gets complicated. Whenever we re-fresh our working bond with Spirit, the dance is simple again.

Easy Does It—Or Does It?

We might sum it up this way—

✧ We are all learning to live in the authentic state of soul freedom and sacred aliveness, and learn we must—but we have free choice about *how* we learn.

✧   The choice is simply whether we learn in a simple, easy and joyous way or in a complicated, arduous and painful way.

Let us explore the journey. Let us explore what is involved in learning to let go and come unconditionally alive, what is involved in allowing the state of soul freedom, sacred aliveness to unfold naturally—*and what it takes to let the journey be a simple, easy and joyous one!*

Chapter 6

Tuning in to Sacred Aliveness

In a comfortable position, with eyes either closed or soft-focus, let yourself gently move into your inner awareness. Let yourself have a few easy, comfortable breaths. Let yourself feel comfortably open for new experience. Gently allowing that your awareness can tune to many things, give your awareness a subtle prompting to move in the direction of body attunement. Let yourself feel your body. Let the experience be easy as you feel your awareness moving into your body, and relaxing there.

Notice that your body is *responsive* to this. Your body responds to your awareness. Let this sense of closeness and responsiveness grow.

Let yourself realize that, as this sense of closeness grows between your conscious awareness and your body state, *you can tune and refine your awareness within your body.*

Refine. Move from the obvious to the subtle. Move from feeling your body as mass, muscle, organs, etc. to feeling the inner plane where life is organized and orchestrated as cells. Tune to the cellular level of your body. Feel the activity, the life processes, the hum of life. Notice that your cells are responsive, your cells respond to your body awareness.

This is a natural and potentially powerful point of communion between body and mind. Every cell is a potent little unit of life with a depth of consciousness, responsiveness, and essential life-intelligence that is, when we tune in to it, both astonishing and welcoming. The cellular level is just the right level to feel the living patterns and patternings of the innate wisdom of the body.

Let's do an experiment.

Suggest to yourself that you don't know where your life really comes from, you don't know for sure that the source of your life is Spirit and even if it is Spirit you're not sure that Spirit blesses you and takes care of you. You don't feel sustained and evolved by a higher reality of infinite good and, disturbing as this is, you feel there's no choice but to buck up on your own, try to survive, and find what happiness your can. You are afraid that your life will not ultimately work out. There is no choice but to live with this core fear.

How do the cells in your body respond to this suggestion? Notice the response.

Relax for a moment, go back to "neutral."

Now suggest to yourself that you can feel the indweling Spirit, you do feel its loving presence, birthing you, blessing you, evolving you. You are free. You know that surviving and finding happiness is not something you have to work out all on your own. You feel sustained in the stream of blessings that is the life of Spirit in you, as you. Over time this grows and grows. Your joy is real. You live in sacred communion with a higher reality of infinite good.

How do the cells in your body respond to this suggestion?

Relax the experiment. Be with yourself for a moment. Let yourself integrate the learning.

Crash Course

Does the life-force in our cells welcome the idea of separation, fear, and compromise? No! Typically, living cells react to that thought program with dissonance, even pain. You may have felt that your cells contracted or even "winced" as you ran that thought program. You may have felt that the natural intelligence of your body's "biocomputer" had a problem even computing the program. You may have felt disoriented or weak or even toxic. These are typical responses.

What is important to realize is that most people, most of the time, are implicitly hurting themselves in precisely this way. They are creating and living with a core stress pattern that, over time, weakens the vital force and invites aging, degeneration and death.

It is easy to really "get it" about this when you do the thought experiment outlined above. You may want to stop and do the experiment again now—or do it whenever you feel receptive to integrate the learning, deeply.

Let yourself have a "crash course" in what is at stake here—

The belief in separation from Spirit
is a toxic stress that literally degenerates
the life-force within us.

Evolutionary Imperative

On the other hand, how does the body's innate intelligence respond to the knowing of oneness with Spirit and infinite good? Typically, our cells respond to this program with resonance and joy. They stir, they thrill, they recognize and affirm that *this is right, this makes sense, this feels good.* And indeed in this state of being we can thrive and evolve into heightened levels of aliveness and well-being. From the biological and cellular point of view—

Living in a state of spiritual communion
is literally imperative
to our wellness and growth.

Renewal

Many workshop participants have remarked that they can tell they'll never be the same after doing this "crash course." That they are no longer swayed by the prevailing thought in our culture that over time we age and lose our vital force. One such participant started calling herself a "walking billboard for sacred aliveness" as she learned to radiate the vitality of cellular communion with Spirit in this way. And truly she is! Anyone who simply looks at Marlene would just know that, if stress is occurring in her life at all, it must be yielding continuously to the spiritual principle of renewal. I find it inspiring just to be in the presence of individuals like her because they take on, beyond the glow of vitality itself, an air of conviction and authority about it all that is deeply confirming—

Life renews and regenerates itself.
A life grounded in Spirit is a life of renewal.

The renewal is simply part of the *"all else shall be added unto us"* that occurs naturally when we seek first the state of spiritual communion.

It's that simple.

Most people probably feel that they are not experiencing profound renewal in their lives, and this would be true simply because they are not seeking spiritual communion in a profound way either.

Spiritual life is meant to be unconditional,
a radical immersion in the unconditonal life of Spirit.

It is inspiring to imagine how utterly our lives can regenerate and renew as we get really saturated in Spirit. But there is a catch here, one on which it is easy to get snagged. The real truth here—that if we seek first the experience of Spirit, all else will be added unto us—can easily lure the conditioned mind to think eagerly of seeing all the things it wants showing up in life. But this reduces the equation to a simplistic platitude, one that just won't lead to much. The equation works when we really understand what is meant by "seek first." I believe that "first" in this expression means *unconditionally*. We are to put Spirit first not just sequentially, but unconditionally. In other words the equation works, and our lives are blessed, renewed and evolved, when we *seek Spirit for the sake of Spirit, not for the sake of what we can get out of it.*

Inner Peace

I saw this vividly in meditation one day when I was working to up-grade the energy state of my frontal aura. I knew that this part of the aura functions much like the prow of a ship in that it "cuts the waters," or interfaces our present reality into our next possibilities. Whatever we carry in our frontal aura can literally inform the world around us as to who we are and what we are available to interact with, what we expect, what we want, what we fear, etc. I was guided in meditation to welcome upgrades for various aspects of my relationship with the world, especially the aspects of sincere, mutual respect, genuine comfort among people, and expectancy of a natural flow of abundance. These energy upgrades were lovely, and I welcomed them with joy. Then the flow of the meditation altered abruptly and my awareness was shifted from the frontal aura experience, taken up through my crown chakra, and taken into a heightened moment of direct communion with the universal presence of Spirit. It was a moment of pure and simple *devotion.* I was prompted to *let go* of my new enthusiasm about drawing abundance, comfort and respect into my relationship with the world. I was held in pure devotion. I was shown how certain it is, and always is, that as we sustain a pure and devoted state of communion with the divine, we don't really have to *worry* about manifesting abundance, comfort—or anything else. We live in a natural state of inner fullness that *transcends need,* yet *draws to us,* paradoxically as it may seem, whatever share of manifest good we are able to receive.

The vividness of this realization, like an "aha" experience, launched me into a growth spiral of discovering and rediscovering and rediscovering, over time, that I could have my comfort supplied to me, moment by moment, as a direct vibrational feature of communing with Spirit. As this way of having comfort grows, it ripens into authentic inner peace, a natural state of inner fullness that, again, transcends need, yet draws to us, in due course, whatever share of manifest good we are able to receive.

All this, of course, can really bring up our issues about trusting and letting go. "Can it really be so simple, so elegant, to live in simple communion with Spirit and have our lives work out? Am I willing to trust?" As we said in Chapter 5, letting go can be arduous and difficult, or it can be exquisitely easy. It becomes a pivotal point of spiritual growth. Learning to *really* trust and *really* let go is the proving ground where we demonstrate our ability to live from higher wisdom. How well have we attuned ourselves, really, to the higher wisdom of life, the wisdom that is bigger than our personal consciousness and knows that life is all there is, the wisdom that knows how to allow life rather than resist life, the wisdom that knows how to seek communion with Spirit, *for the sake of Spirit,* and let all else be added as it may?

Learning to live in attunement is not something that can be forced—that's when it starts to feel maddeningly difficult. Greater attunement occurs naturally when our awareness is *refined.* We'll have more to say about refinement as we proceed. *Easy does it.*

For myself, tuning in to the spiritual dimension of things has become more or less a way of life, keeping me in a growth spiral of learning to trust and let go, learning to find renewal, learning, as best I can, how these things work. Many who know me have marveled at how readily I let go of worldly things, for example, when the winds of change blow through my life. I love being a "home-body" with a nurturing home setting to anchor my work in the world—yet I have frequently, through the years, been prompted to let go of all that and "float" from place to place as I seek to co-create, with the universal Spirit, my right expression in the world. And so the places to call home, the furnishings and the houseplants, the familiarity and the comfort, freely come and go through the years as I keep getting my lessons on letting comfort and peace grow from within. As for renewal and rejuvenation, I find that most individuals who don't happen to know my chronological age take me for 10–15 years younger than my actual years. I am certain this flows from the spiritual lifestyle. I have come to believe that—

There is a kind of sacred alchemy
that wants to take over in the human body
when we relinquish the idea that we are separate from divine Source,
when we give ourselves a chance
to host the living presence of Spirit in our bodies.

Quantum Reality

I'll never forget a workshop in Sebastopol, California when, as I facilitated group exploration of body-mind-Spirit, I felt a powerful "energy prompting" to really claim the human body as a shrine of Spirit. I always lead workshops by giving words to what there is energy for in the moment, and at that moment the energy wanted it said, emphatically and succinctly, that *"The body is not meant to be governed by the laws of the physical plane."*

The statement created quite a stir. People perked up as if to say "Really?" It was almost as if they were rousing out of some sort of trance. I realized then how much we tend to be influenced—practically entranced—by the age-old mass consensus or belief system that sees human life as locked into an immutable physical world with built-in laws and limitations such as aging, mortality, karma, even linear time itself. I realized that—

✧ We are not governed by the laws of the physical plane *unless we believe that we are.*
✧ In fact, we are never governed by an external reality—we are always governed by our inner beliefs.

This of course is precisely what quantum physics has come to understand about quantum particles—that they behave like physical matter if that's how we expect them to behave, but they behave like energy waves if *that's* how we expect them to behave. (More about this as we proceed.)

So the question arises: if a person believes that he is governed by the laws of the physical world, is he then governed by the laws of the physical world—or is he merely governed by his *belief* that he is governed by the laws of the physical world? This is not a tease question. Think about it.

As you think about it you realize that there is no difference, that, quite literally, *the physical world around us and our beliefs about it are not two different things.* The physical world is the outer arena of thought, reflecting back to us what's going on in the inner arena of thought, i.e. in our consciousness.

For example, the physical body gets depleted and sick to reflect back to us our thoughts and beliefs about loss and suffering and limitation. Or our physical world threatens us and hurts us to reflect back to us our thoughts and beliefs about unsafety and weakness and limitation.

The key element in these scenarios is limitation—a limiting world reflects limiting thought.

What is the world? The world is a living plasma of responsive energy imprinted and directed by our thought. The world is an arena of infinite possibilities selectively participated in and potentiated by what's going on in our consciousness.

These possibilities are, themselves, energy. They are *pre-physical.* We can draw them into physical manifestation by our thought if we in fact invest the thought. This is always up to us, not just as individuals but, especially, as participants in mass consciousness and mass consensus. I once heard a physicist state that particles show up as physical matter because everyone expects them to, but that, if no one expected them to manifest physically, they would stay in the pre-physical dance of energy—and there would be no physical matter. Spiritual sources point to the same truth. *A Course in Miracles,* for example, suggests that the world around us would not necessarily need to show up as physical at all, were it not for our thoughts and beliefs in limitation. (There are, of course, many populations in this multi-dimensional universe who have not manifested physical bodies or third-dimensional worlds to inhabit simply because their thought patterns have not compressed to the corresponding levels of fear and limitation.)

Again, the key word is limitation.

Sacred Aliveness

Let's tune in again. Our consciousness is much like a tuning instrument that can tune in to anything. The biggest key to using this instrument well is to *refine* it.

We refine when we let go.

We refine when we allow.

Refine now. Let go of any limiting thought or feeling about the body. Allow that your body, like the particles in quantum physics, is as much a dance of living energy as it is solid matter. Settle into your body awareness. Feel the responsiveness of your body. Breathe.

Tune and refine, as before, to the inner plane where life hums and vibrates and organizes itself as cells.

Allow your cells to be in their own natural state. Take no thought. Be with your cells, allowing, allowing, refining, refining. Let yourself be so open, so allowing, that noticing the natural state of aliveness in your cells, now, is not a mental process, it is a communing. Deeply and fully, commune. *Be* in the life of your cells. Feel life as your cells feel life. *Be* life as your cells are life.

How does this aliveness feel?

Sacred. Simply, sacred. This aliveness is the life of Spirit—in your body *as your body.*

This sacred aliveness is the light of Spirit, shimmering in your cells as the glow of your cellular life-force. It is the breath of Spirit, breathing life in your cells as your cellular life process. It is the power and the joy and the very will of the Source of life swelling in you, as you.

It is the peace of Spirit, abiding in you now as your peace.

Most of all it is the love of Spirit, doing all that divine love does. It is divine love swelling with the passion and bliss of its own rapturous nature and expressing itself by manifesting new forms—like you and I and every one of our cells and every particle in our cells and, really, every form throughout the manifest worlds—to embody its joy. It is divine love holding its manifestations dear and blessing them with all that Spirit is. *Love. Light. Creative Power. Joy. Peace. Wisdom. Beauty. Pure unconditional aliveness. Infinite good. Wholeness.*

Allow. Allow that divine love *is blessing you now.* Not just theoretically, not in some ideal time or some ideal state such as "enlightenment," but now.

Commune in this.

"KISS"

Moments of authentic spiritual communion like this are, simply, sacred. The rest of our moments are times when it is important to *keep it sacred.* Sacred aliveness is unconditional. Coming alive in sacred aliveness must be unconditional—yet we often think of coming alive in the sacred as a special experience that is reserved for special, "spiritual" moments. The old acronym "kiss" for "keep it simple, stupid" needs to be adapted for our times to—

Keep it simply sacred.

Life is sacred, every moment is meant to be sacred. No moments are particularly more spiritual than others, for spirituality is not a part of life or a compartment of life, it is the totality of life.

And our cells already know this. Our cells can reveal to us the sacredness of life, as they experience it, any time we choose to tune in to them in their natural state. Left to themselves, without us needing to introduce a spiritual thought program or to manage it or to monitor it, our cells naturally subsist in an exquisite state of sacred aliveness.

Chapter 7

Higher Mind

Isn't it interesting that, whereas the first exercise in Chapter 6, the "crash course" exercise, revealed a critical link between thought and the body, with intentional thoughts of spiritual attunement yielding the experience of sacred aliveness within the body state, the second or "take no thought" exercise deliberately leaves thought out of the equation—and yet the body has no problem yielding the experience of sacred aliveness to us, seemingly all by itself.

Does this mean that mind does not give shape and direction to the body after all?

It simply means that there is a Higher Mind—and that this Higher Mind gives shape and direction to all things, including our conscious minds, our bodies, and all aspects of our lives, whenever and to whatever extent we allow it to do so by aligning ourselves to its living truth.

We align ourselves to the living truth of Higher Mind when we refine.

In the "crash course" approach what we are refining is *thought* or *mental activity,* as we move from thoughts of separation and fear to thoughts of oneness and freedom and joy. Vibrationally, the latter thoughts are much more refined. In fact we could define "refined" as *closer to the truth* or *closer to the whole.* So whenever we cultivate thought that favors living truth, we are prompting and reminding ourselves to let the Higher Mind direct our lives.

In the "take no thought" approach we refine not thought or mental activity, but the *mind itself,* directly. What refines the mind directly is to simply let go. Letting go allows the mind to tune to its ground state of being, to the state of living wisdom or living truth. We transcend any restriction or distortion or resistance in our conscious awareness and merge directly with the pure living truth of Higher Mind.

The point is that the living truth is really there, in every moment, as the ground state of our being. We can tune into it by refining our thought or by refining our awareness directly—either approach will work and it ultimately doesn't matter how much we favor one aspect of the journey or the other, for Higher Mind shall draw us into the living truth of our being as surely as a lighthouse draws a ship seeking harbor.

The Body Responds to Higher Laws

It is Higher Mind that knows, as it came through that day in the Sebastopol workshop, that the physical body is not meant to be strictly limited by the laws of the physical plane.

A close acquaintance of mine, Barb, tells of a time when she "untwisted" her ankle. She was walking along an uneven terrain and her foot slipped on a loose rock. In that moment her ankle wrenched and twisted. The pain was immediate. But Barb had the presence of mind, the refinement of mind, to realize that in this quantum energy world of ours *nothing is locked in.* She realized that *the flow of linear time itself is not locked in.* She found herself going back in time to just before the ankle had twisted, modifying the flow of time, and proceeding along a course in which the ankle did not twist after all. Just like that, the ankle was fine—no swelling, no pain, as good as if it had never twisted!

Another friend, Sola, tells of a time she was sunbathing on a rock at the banks of a little river in a secluded part of the Mt. Shasta wilderness. The warmth of the sun felt so inviting and the area was so secluded that Sola decided it was safe to strip down and bask in the sun nude. She relaxed languorously into the experience. After awhile she was roused by the sound of men's voices. She looked upstream and saw that three men in a canoe had rounded a bend in the river and were rapidly approaching her spot. As far as she could tell they had not noticed her yet, but within a second or two their canoe would be directly in front of Sola's rock and the men would be certain to see her. Sola knew she didn't have time to scramble for cover. Her Higher Mind rallied. *Nothing is locked in. The physical manifestation of the body itself is not locked in.* Sola instinctively chose to let her body slip into the pre-physical planes of energy. Just that fast the boat was sliding past Sola's rock, the men were just a few yards away from Sola and looking right at her—but they did not see her! Sola had made herself invisible in that moment.

Another acquaintance, Dennis, has unblocked his conscious mind so well that he has become remarkably clairvoyant. He sees what's really going on.

He tells the story of a time when he was on Mt. Shasta with a young mother and her little boy. The woman was doing her best to enjoy conversation with Dennis while also keeping an eye on her boy as he explored the rocks and pathways of his little mountain playground. The little boy saw the rocks as much like the swings and slides and jungle gyms at the playground in town, for these rocks were about the same height and they looked fun to play on.

At a certain point the mother's vigilance lapsed, the boy clambered to the top of a rock, teetered at its edge, and fell. The mother shrieked as she ran to him. She feared the worst. Her child had landed head-first on solid rock. But as she examined him it was clear that the little boy was just fine. "It's a miracle!" she exclaimed. She could hardly believe that he had not sustained head injury.

But Dennis had seen what really happened. When the boy's head struck the base of the rock it *was* injured. Massively. But just that fast, the boy's guardian angel had rushed in and repaired the damage. The healing occurred instantaneously. By the time the mother reached her child he was fine. As Dennis saw it, the child was simply not "signed up," as a soul, to encounter serious injury at that time—though the mother was apparently signed up to explore the "miraculous"—and so the flow of physical plane occurrences needed to be modified by the intervention of Spirit. *Nothing is locked in.*

Reality Is Open

These stories are dramatic. But they illustrate a principle that we can apply in daily life at any time. *Reality is open.* Whatever is manifesting in our lives is open to change by the laws of Spirit.

The part of us that knows this, and knows how to do it, is the Higher Mind.

The Screen of the Mind

Imagine that your ordinary daily awareness is like a computer screen and that at any given moment the screen is displaying your sense of what is going on in your life and of how you're feeling. The display is formatted by your sense of the fundamentals or "abc's"—

- ✧ Agendas
- ✧ Beliefs
- ✧ Conditions

that you feel need to be in place for you to feel good (see Chapter 3), and by a running account of how well you feel your abc's are being satisfied. The display also shows current perturbations in the layered feelings—

- ✧ Judgment
- ✧ Anger and hurt
- ✧ Disappointment and sadness
- ✧ Neediness
- ✧ Inadequacy
- ✧ Fear
- ✧ Separation and aloneness

that drive your conditional search for happiness (again, see Chapter 3). Also shown are contingencies, strategies, and comparative success estimates that the conditioned mind likes to keep an eye on.

All your moments of joy and satisfaction are displayed too, but the display is formatted by your basic program, your abc's of personal happiness, and so all your moments of joy and satisfaction register as inherently conditional or limited. Ultimate happiness never seems to register.

Refresh

Imagine that up in a corner of your screen is a button marked "Refresh."

When you click this button, the display on your awareness screen changes radically. It shifts from conditioned mind format to Higher Mind format and shows you all the principles of living truth by which your life is meant to be guided. It shows you, for example, that—

✧ Life is all there is, infinite, oceanic, and sacred.

✧ Life must evolve.

✧ Individual life is simply the evolutionary play and interplay of infinite divine potentials.

✧ True happiness is unconditional.

✧ Happiness is what you are, not what you need.

✧ The divine will of Spirit is for you to come alive in the most natural state of unconditional soul freedom and sacred aliveness.

✧ Your true inner being subsumes all having and all good. Whatever is truly good for you, you have.

✧ Your body responds to higher laws and subsists naturally in a God-given state of sacred aliveness.

✧ Renewal occurs naturally as you seek the unconditional state of spiritual communion.

✧ Reality is open. Whatever is manifesting in your life is open to change by the laws of Spirit.

✧ Divine love is manifesting you in form and blessing you with all that Spirit is.

All principles of living truth can open to you when you activate the "Refresh" function and access the Higher Mind. And they are available holographically—that is, each principle reveals all the others, participates in all the others, and ultimately contains all the others. Focusing on any one of them can take you into the whole realm of living truth, as every point contains the whole. And likewise, opening into the realm of truth, as a whole, can yield precisely that point of living truth that is meaningful and germane, even illuminating, to the precise moment.

This is the realm of the Higher Mind.

Access

So how do we work the Refresh button? How do we access the Higher Mind?

There are two essential points. We must—

✧ Keep it simply sacred, and
✧ Surrender to the present moment.

Keep It Simply Sacred

Higher Mind is universal. It imprints or blueprints all things with living truth. It is the "One Mind" in the old Buddhist expression, "Wherever there is mind, there is the One Mind." It is always present. And it functions, like all things universal and sacred, by its own natural authority and grace, without effort. *Attuning* to this Mind is meant to be natural and effortless too. Putting forth effort to achieve the state of Higher Mind would be missing the point. Keep it simple, keep it sacred.

The "KISS" approach, of course, runs contrary to the conditioned mind's tendency to invest effort in its agendas, beliefs, and conditions. What is important to realize is that whereas the conditioned mind tends to function as a system unto itself, tense, self-involved, and ultimately self-exhausting, the Higher Mind always functions as part of a larger whole. Higher Mind functions very much like a neuron in a grand, cosmic brain. Just as we would never see one neuron invent its own self-serving program in rebellion to the greater wisdom of the whole brain, our experience of Higher Mind always flows naturally in service to the sacred authority and grace of the universal One Mind.

Retraining our personal awareness habits to access the Higher Mind becomes a subtle matter. So easily, we can find ourselves reaching for the Higher Mind experience—but the reaching, itself, can involve subtle effort and so block the experience. Meanwhile, *Higher Mind is there all along.* It is always present. It's just not showing up on our mental screen when we are held, however subtly, in conditioned mind habits like neediness, investment, or effort.

Changing our awareness habits becomes a training ground for some serious letting go.

Letting go, as we have learned, can be arduous and difficult or exquisitely easy. I believe we finally learn to let it be easy as we learn to favor *refinement* in our awareness habits. Refined awareness gives us a "leg up" on letting go.

Refined means closer to the truth, closer to the reality of Higher Mind that is already there. We refine when we allow. Elusive as this may be for the conditioned mind to grasp, *we don't have to reach for the Higher Mind experience—we simply allow it.*

Another way to say this: we must learn to let our experience of Higher Mind be an action *of* the Higher Mind, not an action of our conditioned mind.

There is a beautiful and effective way to practice this point. Simply repeat to yourself the time-honored expression—

> *Peace, be still. Peace, be still.*
> *Be still and know that I am God.*

These words have a powerful effect, an uncanny ability to calm the mind, remind us to keep it simply sacred, and refresh our awareness into the living truth of the Higher Mind.

Easy does it.

Surrender to the Present Moment

Higher Mind is timeless. It imbues all moments with living truth and makes each moment a mystical threshold or window into the "all that is." We call such a moment the eternal Now. We find our way into this threshold experience when we truly and deeply surrender ourselves into the present moment. As we do this we transcend the time-bound strategies of the conditioned mind and free our awareness from the normal claims of linear time. We move into a present that is not shaped by the past. We move into a present that is not limited by the past. We move into an eternal Now moment of infinite privilege, in which our reality is shaped by Source, by the infinite Spirit.

Soul Freedom

Many years before I learned to use computers and software features like "Refresh" buttons, I was very focused on this whole style of radical spiritual freedom. This was at a time when I lived in Santa Cruz, California. I used to love driving around Santa Cruz in my "Santa Cruisin'" vehicle, an old Mercury with a moonroof, and practice my moment-to-moment awareness of spiritual freedom. I came up with a little visual aid, an earlier version of the Refresh button idea: I would reach to the dashboard and reset the odometer to all zeroes, reminding me that in the life of the Higher Mind there is no linear time and there is no past, there is only the eternal Now. Each

time I saw all those zeroes I was "re-minded" that in each present moment we start fresh. I reached out and worked that reset button every
time I thought of it. It became to me a rousing gesture of freedom
and joy. Each time, I reset my awareness to Now—to the free and clear
present—and refreshed my knowing that as far as Spirit was concerned I was free to draw infinite good into my moment. Spirit would
never put limits on how much good can flow into each moment.

I took it as a sign that I was catching on when, after several months
of this, the odometer broke and stayed set on all zeroes! *Voila.*
Now I had an ongoing reminder of my freedom—and it wasn't up to
me anymore. It was becoming, in its little "visual aid" way, unconditional. The Higher Mind perspective, after all, is that true freedom,
like all things real and enduring and truly of Spirit, is unconditional,
true for all times.

Higher Mind knows that we are always free and we can always
have our highest good. We are free to live consciously in our divinely
endowed state of inner good, which is unconditional, and so to attract
from the world around us the purest possible reflections of our good.
The key is to live fully in the present moment. *Every Now moment
really is a moment of infinite privilege.*

Intention

I believe that human awareness is endowed with just the right tool
for refreshing or re-setting itself to the state of Higher Mind. This tool
enables us to make the shift in such a way that the principles of—

✧ Keep it simply sacred, and
✧ Surrender to the present moment

are naturally and elegantly involved. The tool is *intention.*

I have always believed that intention—when it is truly empowered by our inner conviction, and truly refined by our inner purity—is technique enough to accomplish most anything in the inner life. I have seen this countless times. When we intend something with inner conviction and inner purity, we have it.

Intending and *having* become practically synonymous.

Intention was the key element in the remarkable experiences of Barb and Sola recounted above. Barb *intended* to adapt the spiritual principle that the flow of linear time is not locked in. Sola *intended* to adapt the spiritual principle that the physical manifestation of the body is not locked in. The outer circumstances—the twisted ankle, the approaching canoe—just tested Barb and Sola's power of intention and, really, the inner purity and conviction that carries intention.

Ultimately, all of our life-experiences, from the most dramatic to the most trivial, are prompting all of us to develop our inner conviction, to develop our inner purity, and, most of all, to develop our inner readiness so that, come what may in the outer conditions of life, we can always rally the power of our intention to live in spiritual freedom and to have our highest good.

Chapter 8

Soul Mission

It was Opening Night at a new healing center near Boulder. My sponsor had bought into a new home there and was inspired to turn part of it into a healing center. She had carried the vision of a center for many years—and now was the time to bring her vision to life. She had invited me to "inaugurate" the center with a workshop on Soul Freedom, Sacred Aliveness.

I flew in from California just in time to get to the center on schedule. I walked into the workshop space—and the place was packed! My sponsor had really succeeded in getting the word out for this one. I learned there were authors, healers, life coaches, a doctor or two, even a pastor among the crowd. The whole place was alive with expectancy.

And it was time to get started.

I prefer to lead workshops without a plan or an outline. No matter what the occasion is, I feel that I am there to facilitate *experience,* spontaneous experience, and that the only authentic way for me to do this is to surrender to the moment, to tune in to the group, and to pick up on the next steps of spiritual awakening for the group as the energy for their next steps "ripens" in higher planes. I get promptings on how to facilitate—and off we go.

What was ripening for the group in Colorado that night? I started tuning in to the moment to find out.

Higher Mind Engages Energy Holistically

Sensing energy is a holistic event, involving many elements and multiple layers. For example, the energy can be picked up on any of its "sensory" surfaces such as—

✧ The visual or clairvoyant facet (for example, seeing colors or seeing energy blockages or seeing images and symbols);

✧ The auditory or clairaudient facet (for example, hearing messages or hearing the names of spirit guides);

✧ The kinesthetic or clairsentient facet (for example, feeling chakras opening or feeling energy blockages yield to healing awareness).

More importantly, beneath the various sensory surfaces lies an affective level, a level of feeling. Even deeper lies a claircognizant level, a core of knowing. All energy experiences contain a wealth of knowing. Conversely, all knowing is wrapped in energy and revealed in energy.

This makes the experience of an energy event alive and dynamic, vibrant with potentials for learning and growing.

Higher Mind functions just so. Higher Mind engages energy events holistically.

✧ Higher Mind can pick up the various sensory facets, as appropriate;

✧ Higher Mind can feel the affective tone of the energy event;

✧ Higher Mind can penetrate to the core knowing within the energy; and

✧ Higher Mind can intuit the potentials for learning and growing within the event.

The process unfolds intuitively. Higher Mind is never merely cognitive or merely rational, but deeply intuitive. And it expresses uniquely in each of us. Each of us, as we awaken, is likely to explore the unique mix of subtle sensing experiences that is appropriate to us—and appropriate to how the Higher Mind can be tuned to serve *through* us. For myself, what has always seemed most appropriate is to move very readily, almost nimbly, to the *core knowing* and to the *intuitive growth potentials* within energy events. I use the sensory surfaces and the affective tones to get me there, but I have relatively little interest in the sensory/affective levels for their own sake.

As I sensed the energy of the Opening Night group in Colorado, it seemed to feature a distinctly affirmative, loving vibration, with an image of a list and an intuitive suggestion of an inward, life-review process. I took my cue—and off we went into a lovely, meditative time of appreciating and affirming the things we love. I led the experience by simply suggesting that each person close their eyes, tune in to their lives, and let the affirmative, loving energy of the moment carry them into a kind of inventory of the things that give beauty, joy and endearment to their lives, all the things that belong on the list of things they love. This felt very heartening and beautiful. People got into it. I glanced at my sponsor—she looked really pleased to be hosting the group experience.

I let the experience grow and waited for my next cues, the next energy shift. In a little while the energy shifted indeed. I was startled at first—for I felt distinctly prompted to ask the group to take the list of things they love and tear it up. Would this go over all right? I wondered. Would the inaugural flavor of the evening be skewed?

Was I misreading the knowing element, the guidance, within the energy shift?

I double checked. *Go ahead,* said the energy. This was a moment for me to choose between letting trust be easy or letting trust be hard. I went with easy and moved right into having the crowd visualize tearing up their lists and throwing them away.

What happened next was extraordinary. The vibration of love in the group grew stronger. *Much* stronger. There we sat without a single accustomed thing to focus our love on but we were rising and expanding in a powerful wave of pure love energy.

Then the energy shifted again. Apparently it was time for this: the vibration of *divine soul* descended into the group. The sacred, true Self. The divine Self.

Unconditional Love

When soul consciousness comes in, it makes everything lucid. It's an experience that finds its way into my workshops in many different ways, often unexpectedly like on this evening, but something about how strikingly the experience was coming through for this group made the learning threshold that we moved into especially powerful.

For myself, every sensory surface of the experience that evening—

- ✧ The rich play of light, light of an extraordinary, soulful purity;
- ✧ The subtle vibration, like a signature, of the words "I Am Present;"

   ✧   The whooshing sense of movement from a higher dimension to the plane of conscious awareness;

and every theme of knowing within the energy—

   ✧   The sense of destiny;
   ✧   The abiding peace;
   ✧   The rich and timeless wisdom base that the soul functions in and tests and owns as it incarnates in time and space;
   ✧   The promise of fulfillment;

—all of this was saturated, in a uniquely lucid way, with one essence vibration, the vibration of love.

Love alone is real, the soul presence was affirming. *And you don't need lists and referencings and affirmations of what to love. Whatever you are entertaining in your human experience, seek the essence, seek the love.*

As I gave voice to the message we moved as a group through the learning threshold. We moved to the place where we could truly see ourselves and each other as, simply, incarnate love.

I am certain that this is how God sees us.

When we see ourselves and each other as God sees us there is such a profound sense of letting go, such a relinquishing of personal will, such a deep and abiding peace. We realize with new clarity that, as the old saying goes, "Whatever the question, the answer is love." We realize that there don't have to be any conditions on the activity of divine love. We realize that, really, loving is meant to be as constant as being. What was gifted into the workshop group that night in Colorado was the freedom to love with the constancy, the peace, and the utter power of our spiritual beingness. We discovered how true it is that *our very soul mission is to love,* that we are literally *commissioned* by the infinite Spirit to love and to explore the creative power of divine love and the transformational power of divine love.

And we saw that, as we are true to our soul mission, we *won't stop* loving.

Since that night I have come to believe that perhaps the best definition of soul that can ever be given is simply this—

Soul is the sacred inner essence of us
that abides in divine love,
is commissioned in divine love,
and, true to its mission, simply will not stop loving.

We will have much more to say about the soul and its mission in subsequent chapters.

Love Bestows Integrity

When we give ourselves the freedom to love unconditionally, when we beckon our sacred, true Self, our divine soul, to take ascendancy in our lives—then, finally, our lives take on a dimension of wholeness or spiritual integrity, the kind of unchanging, unwavering, bedrock integrity that only pure unconditional love can bestow.

For divine love, it turns out, has everything to do with integrity.

Divine love, ultimately, is the very passion of Spirit to be, and to be in form. Anything that "be's" can do so only on the basis of a coherent, fundamental integrity of form and—

Divine love,
the essential passion of Spirit to be and to express,
bestows this fundamental integrity of form.

Put more simply, love binds things together and holds things together. Love is the unifying principle of the universe. Love harmonizes, love literally holds things together. Love is the essential spark, love is the synergy within all form.

Awakening to this, directly sensing the inner workings of divine love within the life of all manifest forms, is a fundamental mystical experience. It is often associated with finding God, or sensing the breath of God, or seeing the signature of the Creator within creation, or finding the sacred aliveness or *shakti* of the indwelling universal Spirit.

This vein of mystical experience often registers, in our times, with the ancient yet contemporary flavor of recognizing the sacred feminine aspect of Spirit, the Divine Mother, blessing and nurturing all of life.

The essence of the experience is love. As we said in an earlier chapter, the chapter on tuning in to sacred aliveness in our bodies, what divine love does is—

   ✧ Swell with the passion and bliss of its own rapturous
      nature;
   ✧ Express itself by manifesting new forms to embody its
      joy; and
   ✧ Hold its manifestations dear by blessing them with all that
      Spirit is—love, light, creative power, joy, peace, wisdom,
      beauty, pure aliveness, infinite good, wholeness.

The greatest of these is love.

What begins in divine love grows naturally into wholeness, for divine love creates wholeness.

Love Creates Wholeness

In the presence of divine love all the parts of life come together in wholeness, in a coherent, formal integrity that is sacred.

In the presence of divine love all the elements of living truth come together holographically, where every part contains the whole and reveals the whole and where the wholeness of living truth, in turn, reveals every part.

In the presence of divine love our senses register wholeness and vibrate in wholeness, our feelings register wholeness and thrill to wholeness, our mind registers wholeness and commands certainty of wholeness, our entire being becomes awash in wholeness.

Love Carries Us Home

In the presence of divine love all the elements of the spiritual journey that we are exploring in this book come together in a coherent whole. The elements of—

- ✧ Allowing life;
- ✧ Letting go;
- ✧ Unconditional aliveness;
- ✧ Natural soul freedom;
- ✧ Havingness;
- ✧ Unconditional happiness;
- ✧ Creative tension;
- ✧ Co-creating;
- ✧ Aligning to divine will;
- ✧ Spiritual communion and renewal;
- ✧ Appreciating the body as a quantum phenomenon of both matter and energy;

- ✧ Tuning to sacred aliveness in the body;
- ✧ Devotion to Spirit for the sake of Spirit, unconditionally;
- ✧ Refining thought and belief;
- ✧ Keeping it simply sacred;
- ✧ Letting our reality be open to change by the laws of Spirit;
- ✧ Accessing Higher Mind;
- ✧ Surrendering to the present moment;
- ✧ Sourcing good into each moment freely and without the constraints of linear time;
- ✧ Intention;
- ✧ Conviction;
- ✧ Purity;
- ✧ Engaging energy holistically;
- ✧ Seeing as God sees;
- ✧ Soul mission

—all these and many other elements that shall find their way into this book are quickened, brought vibrantly to life, and drawn powerfully together in a coherent holistic spiritual path, a path that grows rich with the sacredness of what life is really about, a soul mission that inspires us, ennobles us and, ultimately, carries us home.

And this soul mission—to explore and master the workings of unconditional love—can unify all the elements of the spiritual journey *easily*.

So if, as we said at the end of Chapter 5, the only real issue is whether we travel the spiritual path with simplicity, ease, and joy or with complication and strain, the surest way to travel the path with simplicity, ease, and joy is to *stay true to love*.

Chapter 9

Staying True to Love

It was mid-August at Mt. Shasta. I had just completed a week-long intensive on the mountain, and I was feeling high, really expansive and full, from facilitating the workshop. It had been a gathering of sixteen awakening souls so inspired to explore "Soul Freedom, Sacred Loving, Sacred Aliveness" that, together, we had become deeply immersed in the profound beauty of the spiritual journey. I felt awash in soul love. I felt awash in wholeness. I was lingering at Shasta with a dear friend, as the rest of the group had disbanded and set off for their homes across the country.

As I relaxed into my free time around town I found myself slipping, to my great surprise, into petty judgments and opinions. Little things about people and their behaviors—an insincere voice, a somber face, a high gasoline price, twangy music in a store—little things like this would irk me and I would go right into judgment. Has nothing really changed in me, I wondered. What happened to the unconditional love I thought I was truly learning to live by? Will any amount of immersion in sacred light and love ever heal this core grumpiness in me?

That evening, we went to a dramatization of the teachings of Jesus put on each year by the St. Germain Foundation based in Mt. Shasta. One particular line from the pageant was so right for me, and

I for it, that it penetrated right to the wounded place in my psyche and started working on me. The line was, "Whatsoever you do to the least of my brothers, you do to Me," a line I had heard, of course, many times before—but not like I was hearing it now.

Sacred Wholeness

Now I was hearing a message about wholeness. *Whatever I do to any part of the whole, I do to the whole.* The "Me" in the expression "Whatsoever you do to the least of my brothers, you do to Me," is the cosmic wholeness. One could call it the mystical Christ, or the infinite Brahmam, or Great Spirit, or any other name one chooses. It is the sacred wholeness of life.

I knew that the path of conscious soul freedom that I was committed to living, or that I thought I was committed to living, confers a natural ability to experience life unconditionally, to experience life beyond boundaries, divisions, and separations, to experience life in its true state, the state of wholeness. I knew, or thought I knew, that the path of conscious soul freedom makes me free to be a conscious part of the whole and a conscious *participant*—and it was precisely this, my personal participation in the sacred wholeness of life, that was being jarred by my petty judgments. I *felt* this, deeply. The learning registered deep in my gut as I saw what was happening to me. I saw that whenever I would slip into judgment I would lose the tangible experience of wholeness. It was just that simple. And whenever I would call myself back from judgment, back to love, I could taste the sacred wholeness of life again, I could feel the exquisite sweetness of pure divine love running evenly through things, bestowing wholeness and lifting me, restoring me, as a part of the whole, in the same exquisite sweetness, the same wholeness. I could *participate* in sacred wholeness again, *consciously.*

It seemed I had set quite a learning for myself—

Any judgment, however subtle, blocks the ability
to consciously participate in the sacred wholeness of life.

My awareness had grown lucid enough, from the week-long workshop, to be able to track the pattern very clearly. I plied the lesson over and over, I coaxed my heart to keep coming back to love, I saw with heightened clarity and a compelling sense of initiation, like a mystical glimpse into the inner mysteries of the cosmic Christ, that—

Wholeness is what is real,
and judgment is just choosing to look away from what is real.

I saw that within the reality of the sacred wholeness of life *there is no "least,"* as in the expression "whatsoever you do to the least of my brothers." Spirit does not see "least." Nor "less"—nor, for that matter, "greater" or "greatest." There is only equality. Equality is an absolute cornerstone of the mystical Christ consciousness. What Spirit sees is wholeness, and, within the wholeness, equal parts, equal vessels of the infinite divine love, all parts subsumed into the whole with equal divine grace, all parts expressing the whole with equal divine grace. So the reference to "least" points to human perception—or *mis*perception. When we perceive anything, anything at all, as "least" or even as "less," we are actually misperceiving, to put it kindly, or, to put it more bluntly, we are looking away from what is real.

Judgment, the act of looking away from what is real, is an act of rebellion or infidelity to the living fabric of sacred wholeness. And it compromises our ability to *experience* the exquisite wholeness that all of life is naturally sustained in.

Spiritual Fitness

Choosing wholeness is one of life's most powerful lessons, and it comes to us in ways that are both humbling and exalting. Each time the lesson occurs we get more spiritually fit. I "learned" these things that particular year at Mt. Shasta but I have needed to *keep* learning them, to carry the learning with me, to deepen the initiation, to let all of life keep exposing the wounded places in my psyche to new rounds of pain and humbling, new windows of compassion and illumination, new opportunities to heal judgment and separation, new opportunities to center in love and stay true to love.

Life has a way of orchestrating these rounds. A powerful—if harrowing—round occurred for me during the rainy El Niño winter in northern California in 1997-1998. That winter, I needed to rally my life-force against an aggressive and very stubborn flu. The flu virus made alarming headway. I felt sicker than I've ever been in my life. As I lay in bed I tuned my awareness, as best I could, to the inner terrain where the battle was raging. I noticed that the flu virus had apparently found a particular nerve in my chest, near the heart, that registered a unique and sickening sensation of *trouble* whenever the virus was making headway. This sensation became, for me, like a calling card or signature of the virus' attack. During phases of feeling sicker this sensation grew more distressing. During phases of feeling better the sensation subsided. I learned to track this distress signal as a way of monitoring how well or how poorly my life-force was meeting the viral challenge. Over time the phases of viral challenge diminished and I moved into the stage of feeling mostly better but not fully recovered, into that delicate time after a tough flu when it feels okay to undertake more activity but only *gingerly*, lest the virus revive.

It was then that I entered a period of extraordinary inner sensitivity. I would be driving around town doing errands, with no particular flu-ish signals flickering in my nerves, and I'd find myself slipping into judgment at the state of California for not maintaining the roads better, whenever I encountered a little pothole or rough spot in the road. Didn't they *know* the El Niño rains were coming this year, I griped in my mind. Didn't they know the roads would take a beating? As soon as I went into judgment, the distress signal would flicker in my chest. Uh oh, I thought, the virus is trying to rally again. But why was the virus making headway just now? *Because my own life-force waned in moments of judgment!* Sure enough, as I let go of judgmental feelings about the road conditions, the distress signal in my chest dissipated. If I went into judgment again the distress signal revived—it was uncanny. The pattern played and replayed for several days with telling consistency. I'll never forget the learning spiral—

Judgment literally weakens the life-force within the body.

Tuning in to Sacred Wholeness

If we're ever feeling unclear or fuzzy about what's at stake here we don't need to "up the ante" by getting sick, we can easily recapitulate the challenge by doing a little inner experimenting similar to the thought experiments given in Chapter 6.

> Tune in to your cells, those responsive little units of life-force and intelligence within you, and feel their response as you suggest to yourself that you seriously question whether this world subsists in sacred wholeness. That as far as you can tell from people and their behavior, it's not at all certain that we are created in divine light or commissioned by divine love. Suggest the same doubt

about yourself. Feel the doubt. Where's the light and love that is supposed to be unifying all of us in a divinely endowed state of beauty and good, you question. Disturbing as it feels, you're deeply uncertain about all this. You see plenty of reasons to hold people, including yourself, in judgment. You are afraid that this core judgment may never resolve.

How do your cells feel as you run this thought program? Do they feel uneasy? Dissonant? Perhaps a bit coarsened, or dumpy, or disgruntled? Does the sense of vital life-force within you become skewed or diminished? These are typical responses.

Now relax your thought process and go back to "neutral" for a moment.

Now suggest to yourself that you can feel the divine light and love within others, and within yourself, you do feel its presence, birthing everyone, unifying everyone, evolving everyone into the highest awakening of the sacred potentials of life, each of us learning to awaken through the specific learning thresholds, opportunities, and challenges that best serve our growth each step of the way. Each of us is doing our best at each moment, our "best" being based, as it must, on precisely what we have learned well so far, what we have learned well enough to build next steps of growth upon. You see the divine order in this. You are willing to bless others, and yourself, for learning to express light and love through the specific opportunities and challenges that they are manifesting in their lives. You are willing to recognize the divine order, the loving guidance of Spirit in this. You sense that the living presence of Spirit is holding all of us in precisely this blessing, the blessing of divine order. You feel naturally grateful for the stream of blessing that is the life of Spirit in you, as you. You are at peace.

How do your cells feel with this thought program? Notice how they stir and respond with resonance and joy, they "cell-ebrate," they swell to affirm the rightness, the inherent wisdom, in this thought program.

As the response grows, every cell in the body, and the body itself, vibrates in its most natural state—simple wholeness, the wholeness of being alive in the same sacred aliveness that sustains all things.

Feel the wholeness of being alive in this way. Feel it freeing your cells to know their innermost truth of fitness and well being. See if you can feel your cells freeing up completely, unconditionally. This is the wholeness of being alive in an aliveness that is unconditional.

Now relax and be with yourself for a moment to integrate the learning here—

    ✧ The state of judgment literally weakens the life-force within us.
    ✧ The state of gratitude and blessing strengthens the life-force within us.
    ✧ True fitness and well being is a simple matter of always participating in the sacred wholeness of life.

All of Life Is a Thought Experiment

If life subsists in wholeness, and conscious living is about participating in wholeness, every relationship becomes an arena in which to work out these principles. The thought experiment given above unfolds these principles in our relationship with the life-force within our own bodies. Other relationships could equally well yield the same principles. In actuality *all of life is a thought experiment,* for, as we said in Chapter 6, the manifest world around us and our beliefs about it are not two different things.

> *The manifest world is the outer arena of thought,*
> *reflecting back to us*
> *what's going on in the inner arena of thought,*
> *that is, in our consciousness.*

The world around us is really just a living plasma of responsive energy imprinted and directed by our thought.

In this view, whatever our consciousness interacts with, all the various aspects of the manifest world into which our thought interfaces, are things with which we have a relationship. For example, we have relationships with—

- ✧ Time
- ✧ Space
- ✧ Money

to name a few especially meaningful examples. (We'll have more to say shortly about these three in particular.) One could easily generate a long list of other things we have relationship with, such as pets and pet care, daily rhythms, work deadlines, angels, history, calories, sexuality, intuition, email, voicemail, prayer and meditation, journaling, childhood, street noise, sound and silence, color and texture, planet earth, oral hygiene, choice-making, karma, aging, politics, tools, toys, traffic laws, traffic lanes, chocolate, dreams—needless to say, it's a very long list. And we haven't even mentioned the intricate world of interpersonal relationships. All relationships are

meaningful. In principle one could explore any relationship and discover, within that relationship, that—

- ❖ Judgment weakens.
- ❖ Gratitude and blessing strengthen.
- ❖ We feel best when we get back to wholeness.

I had a vivid chance to learn about this when I first moved to Santa
Cruz. In my inner vision I was picturing myself finding a rental in
some secluded and scenic setting outside the city. But nothing like
this seemed to be available and, after several weeks of searching, I
settled for an apartment in town. In my consciousness, however, I
still envisioned a "dream home" in the country. A couple of weeks
went by. Then one day, in the middle of a telephone reading/healing
session I was doing for a client, a furious pounding came on the front
door of my apartment. At first I chose to not answer, not wanting to
interrupt the session. But whoever was knocking wouldn't go away.
Finally I went to the door.

It was my new landlord, and he looked enraged. "How come your
check bounced?" he demanded.

There was no reason at all for my check to have bounced, so I
assured him of that. "Surely this can be cleared up," I said. "I really
can't take the time right now, though, because I simply must take
care of my client, I can't leave her dangling in the middle of a session.
Can I call you when I'm finished? That'll be within the hour."

He said he wouldn't be home for several hours and stormed away
in fury.

What is this really about, I wondered as I went back to my work
space. I had no issue with the landlord. I had no issue with the inter-
ruption. I was happy to hold the incident in an attitude of blessing
as I went back into my phone session. When the phone session was

over I had some free time before I could contact the landlord. And I
didn't know *what* he was up to. Just in case he was thinking of asking
me to leave, I decided to buy a newspaper and check the classifieds.
As soon as I opened the paper to the rentals section my eyes went
right to one particular ad, *"Secluded Country Cottage,"* and I dialed
the number. They were home. They had just placed the ad. I was the
first caller. I drove out and had a look at the place—it was just what
I wanted, a tasteful, modern cottage, very secluded, with a gorgeous
view of wooded hills and, off in the distance, the blue Pacific.

Needless to say, I jumped at the chance to rent such a wondrous
place. Later on, when I finally got to talk with my first landlord, in
town, he explained that earlier that day he had gone to his bank to
withdraw some cash for spending money but had been told that he
couldn't have any cash because, said the teller, a check from a certain
Mark Schoofs had bounced making the account overdrawn. Apparently the landlord was humiliated to be denied a little cash in his
home bank, and he had charged straight to me in anger. *That's when
the window opened.* Before the day was over the bank explained that
the teller had spoken inaccurately, that my check was merely "uncol-
lected," which of course is very different than "nonsufficient funds."
*By then I had moved through the window, found my greater good
awaiting me, and embraced it.* It all happened fast. The first landlord
was willing to release me from the apartment in town, and I moved
into my dream cottage in the hills outside Santa Cruz.

Time, Space, and, Quirkily, Money Too

I've often marveled at how easily the universe manifested that window. As the facts were straightened out there wasn't a single good
reason for me to have been looking into the classified ads that day.

And yet, in the relationship between my inner vision and time, space, and, quirkily, money too, there was every reason for me to find that cottage that day. The universe, great teacher that it is, did offer me a reason to look away from the window: I certainly could have gone into judgment, anger at the landlord, anger at the bank, anger at "the system," etc. I could have reacted in fear rather than blessing the incident with a view to discovering what it was really about for me. I am certain that, had I reacted in judgment, anger, or fear, the whole incident would have led to a different outcome than it did.

The universe is always reckoning with what's going on inside of us and responding in subtle, unforeseeable ways. Yes, this is meant to keep us alert. This is meant to keep us open to the learning and growing thresholds in every new moment. This is meant to keep us free of judgment, to keep us willing to bless whatever is going on and, ultimately, to keep us choosing to stay true to love.

Choosing Love

It's one thing to say we're not going to slip into judgment anymore, but another to practice it. We all have our opinions. We all have our likes and dislikes. And spiritual evolution will not necessarily change them. As some one once said, if you don't like okra now, that's not likely to change when you're enlightened. I suspect that I personally will never care for twangy music in stores. We could all make our lists. And the lists are valid. They express the uniqueness, the richness and diversity of being human. No one would want to live in a world where everyone likes exactly the same things, anyhow.

But staying true to love is not about liking everything.

✧   Liking is a human emotion.

✧ Loving, on the other hand, is a spiritual constant, an absolute feature of our spiritual beingness itself. Love is what we are in our beingness, not what we entertain in our emotions.

Staying true to love is not about disliking nothing—but it *is* about *judging nothing.*

✧ Disliking is a human emotion.

✧ Judging is a denial of Spirit. Judging is an act of personal will straying from divine will and seeking to fracture the unified sacred wholeness of life. As we said earlier, sacred wholeness, the unified presence of the living Spirit indwelling all of us, is the only reality. Judgment is the rebellious choice to look away from this one reality.

Love Is Unconditional
or It's Not Love at All

Is it possible, then, to dislike something or some one and yet not judge them? Yes, it is. Is it possible to even *love* what we don't like? Yes it is. And does our soul mission—to explore and master the workings of unconditional love—include learning to love the people and things that we don't really like? It certainly does. No soul ever came to this planet on the condition that it would only have to work on loving the people and things that are easy to love.

We commonly mistake endearment for love. We take satisfaction and comfort in feeling close to the people and things we've become endeared to. It's easy to do this. Yet this very pattern of endearment tends to set the human psyche up to distrust whatever is *different* from the things we've grown endeared to. For example, when people are endeared to their country or their religion or their politics, their way of life or their way of looking at life, they may distrust other ways, other peoples, etc. Intolerance can ensue, even hostility—it's a sad but familiar tale. There is no true love here. When "love" becomes conditional and restricted, it is not love at all, it is merely endearment. Authentic love, the real thing, like all things truly of Spirit, is *unconditional, unrestricted, and universal.*

And our greatest value, we need to remember, is this authentic love, itself, not the things we try to attach it to, no matter how dear they may be. *Our greatest value is the love.*

Love is also commonly confused with getting our needs met. We "love" our friend or our partner or our spouse when connecting with them fills our needs. But if they start failing to behave in the ways that we've decided we need them to behave, we may react in anger, hurt and blame. It's another sad but familiar tale. There is no true love in such "love/hate" relationships. Again, *true love is unconditional—or it's not love at all.*

Love is a radical subject.

In fact, when we really understand the nature of unconditional love we realize that—

> *If we're not loving everyone and everything*
> *we're not really loving anyone or anything.*

Love doesn't pick and choose. Love does not exclude.

Letting Love Live in Us, as Us

How can we love everyone and everything, inclusively and unconditionally? It sounds so ideal and abstract.

First of all, it is not up to us to generate the love. Spirit does that part. Spirit sources and supplies an unlimited flow of love. This is the nature of Spirit. As the old expression goes, "God is love." This is literally true. Our job is to simply tune ourselves to divine love, to *allow* divine love, to be open vessels of it and to let it live in us, as us. It is really so simple.

But if we complicate things by trying to generate the love on our own we miss the whole point—*and* we set ourselves up for the deepest and subtlest judgment of all, the judgment that is easiest to slip into, which is judgment of self. "Why am I not more loving? What's wrong with me?" This of course is how all the judgment starts. As we know, all the drama of separation anxiety and separation wounding, all the layered judgment, anger, hurt, sadness, neediness, inadequacy, and fear—it all starts with not being okay with self.

Meanwhile, all along, our "yoke" is meant to be light and easy, simple and sacred. It was never up to us to generate the love—Spirit does that part. Good news! Our job is simply to tune ourselves to the reality of love within us, to *allow* it, and to let it *live* in us, as us.

Recall the description of what divine love does, given in Chapters 6 and 8.

Divine love—

- ✧ Swells with the passion and bliss of its own rapturous nature;
- ✧ Expresses itself by manifesting new forms to embody its passion and bliss; and
- ✧ Blesses these manifest forms by endowing them with all that Spirit is—love, light, creative power, joy, peace, wisdom, beauty, pure unconditional aliveness, infinite good, sacred wholeness.

Abstract as these three points may seem, the third gives a concrete handle. *Love blesses.*

Love Blesses

Love's nature is to bless. It starts with divine love, the infinite Being-ness that we call Spirit, blessing its manifestations—you and I and everyone everywhere—with a full share in all that Spirit is. When *we* bless, we simply *recapitulate what Spirit is already up to.* We *join in* with what Spirit is doing. We participate, we see as God sees. We see everyone as a *child* of God, blessed and endowed with spiritual love, light, creative power, joy, peace, wisdom, beauty, pure unconditional aliveness, infinite good, sacred wholeness—all that God is. We allow this refined perceptual awareness as an act of fidelity to the divine order. It's our way of saying, If Spirit's nature is to bless, may Spirit do so *through us*, through our perception and through our aware-ness. We let ourselves see the divine order working in the life of every one of us, lovingly carrying us along a path of awakening, and living, and even ultimately mastering, our perfect divine endowment of light and love and goodness and *all* the attributes of Spirit.

This way of seeing takes us into a deep and abiding peace. We cen-ter in this. We keep our consciousness simple, sacred, centered in this knowingness of infinite blessing. We surrender. We feel the timeless perfection of divine will. We let our consciousness be aligned and held in the timeless perfection of divine will. We bless as God blesses.

Bless as God Blesses

Such a state of blessing is constant and unchanging. It never wavers. It is always there. In fact it is there *before anything ever happens.*

True blessing flows freely and unconditionally—it does not wait to see what's going to happen, examine things as they happen to see if they merit blessing, and then bless them accordingly. True blessing simply blesses. Freely, unconditionally, constantly.

True blessing pre-empts judgment.

True blessing sustains us in wholeness.

Back to Innocence

The habit of unconditional blessing frees our awareness to see each other in our true innocence. We learn to see everyone, ourselves included, as truly innocent—as needing nothing more, nothing more at all, than to simply work out the remembrance of who we really are.

Who We Are Is Enough

And we learn to recognize that who we are is enough. We are parts of the sacred whole. We carry the sacred whole within us. All the divine potentials of life lie within us. Within our divine nature we carry, for example, the essence of happiness. This means that the essential benefit and reward that would flow from having any and all of our true desires met—simply, happiness, feeling good, feeling fulfilled—is something that we already have. We have the essence of peace too, and of power and wisdom and beauty—*all that flows to us from Spirit is ours, absolutely ours to awaken and live, as long as we understand its source and participate in its source.* This is the original blessing, the cosmic blessing, that Spirit is already pouring itself into us, as us, so that we might experience Its sublime nature and share in Its sublime nature.

What Can Be Added?

This raises a compelling question. If our life is really the sublime, ineffable life-stream of Spirit, flowing in us as us—what can be added to that? In the time-honored teaching that as we seek first the kingdom of Spirit all else will be added unto us, *what can be added?*

Ordinary human awareness believes that a great many things need to be added. We want to eat well, we want to live in a nice place, we want to be paid well for doing meaningful work, we want honor and recognition and friendship and health, we want to have a good time when we go to the park or the beach or the ballgame or the movies, etcetera, etcetera. But when our human awareness gets caught up in seeking all these things it can slip too easily into investing in its perception of need. It's as if the more energy we invest, the more "return" we think we'll get. As we've seen in an earlier chapter on the conditioned mind, this style of awareness tends to block the authentic experience of happiness—

And if we don't experience true and fulfilling happiness
when the things we want come into our lives,
have they really been added?
Have we really received them?

Conditioned human awareness struggles with this existential doubt and misgiving. The conditioned mind wonders whether we're missing out, or going about things all wrong, or somehow missing the point.

Reflections

Ultimately, only one thing can be added to the life of Spirit in us as us—

Reflections.
Reflections of the ineffable sacred aliveness
that is living and evolving in us, as us.

Reflections—chances to see yet more clearly and appreciate yet more deeply that this sacred aliveness is who we really are. Chances to see and appreciate, in the proving ground of real human experience, the utter divinity of who we really are.

The kingdom of the living Spirit is *within* us. As we learn, and learn well, to seek first this living divinity within ourselves, all of the various good things that can be "added" in the outer arena of our lives gain a dimension of ultimate meaningfulness by reflecting back to us, as they are meant to, our own indwelling divinity. They reflect our goodness. They reflect our light. They reflect our wisdom and peace, our power and beauty. Paramahansa Yogananda once said "When you see something of great beauty, close your eyes and realize that the source of that beauty is within you." The whole dance of the manifest worlds is beckoning us to the Source of the dance within. When we go to the park or the beach or the ballgame or the movies, we enjoy the experience to the extent that we let it stimulate our inner joy and reflect our inner joy and wellness, the authentic, unconditional, spiritual state of joy that can, in turn, manifest as our relative human joys, but *only* when our inner joy is in place, *only* when we have really *owned* our inner nature. This is the real pleasure of life. Pleasure-seeking in our society has become an ever-growing obsession with ever-more stimulating outer experience, but the real pleasure of life is a simple, mellow state of illumined inner awareness that hums along in its own essential, constant inner joy while finding, as it may, greater and greater waves of outer joy in the reflections, in the outer dance of our lives.

The dance of life beckons us, most of all, to find the reflections of our love. We need these reflections. We need to know that we are beings of love, and that our ultimate value is this priceless divine love, endowed into each of us as us. We need to see our successes and pleasures, our homes and health and friends and futures and *all* the things we value, as reflecting the priceless inner value of who we really are as beings of love.

Love Is How We Perfect the Art of Coming Unconditionally Alive

Love is the key. In fact, love is how we perfect the art of coming radically alive, unconditionally alive. When we learn to let pure divine love live in us, as us, then we are unconditionally alive. And then we are ready, then we are worthy.

> *When we are letting pure divine love live in us, as us,*
> *then all else can be added unto us.*

Then the universe can see us as worthy of new adventures, new openings, new invitations to explore greater and greater good. Then the universe sees, "Oh, there's some one who understands how it works—let's give *them* more."

Love Carries Us Home

As we turn on the spiral of greater and greater good, as we explore new reflections at this turn and that turn, centering each new reflection in the impeccable inner goodness and love of who we are, the sacred wholeness of life blossoms and matures.

In sacred wholeness, all parts fit. Each new moment feels just right. Each new development feels exquisitely right, welcome, illumining, satisfying, like a master stroke by a master Artist. We sense the Artist, more and more, in all the reflections. We sense the sacred Higher Presence of cosmic divine life.

And *getting closer to this* is what we seek when we seek anything at all.

Dharma

We are drawn to each other because we sense the presence of the sacred in each other. We are drawn to each other to gain reflections of the sacred in each other. We bless each other by providing these reflections. We bless each other when we incarnate our divinity.

> *We all have a fundamental duty or dharma,*
> *a universal "job description,"*
> *which is simply to incarnate divinity.*

We incarnate divinity when we come alive unconditionally, when we "live from the Source" and let the infinite Spirit live in us, as us. As we incarnate our divinity passionately and well, our brother or sister can see the reflection of their own divinity.

Divine Plan

In all of this, there is freedom. Nothing needs to be added to who we already are—incarnations of an infinite Source. And each of us is free, fully enfranchised to unfold the potential that flows into us from the infinite Source. In this state of freedom, no one needs to seek love, light, creative power, joy, peace, wisdom, beauty, aliveness, wholeness, or any other form of good from anyone else. Everyone carries what they need inside, everyone carries the kingdom of the living Spirit within them. Granted, we really appreciate getting the *reflections* of our divine nature from each other—it's hard to imagine awakening our full potential without the help of others.

But these reflections add to our good only as we are doing the essential inner work, only as we are learning to own the infinite good that is our true inner nature.

All of this is meant to flow and unfold *freely*. We are meant to live in a free and open universe of unconditional blessing. This is the divine plan. It is a plan of—

✦ Absolute soul freedom; and
✦ Unconditional sacred aliveness.

Chapter 10

Blessing, Gratitude, and the Rhythm of Awareness and Healing

In this free and open universe of unconditional blessing, where we are free to flow with the divine plan and to in fact complete the divine plan by participating consciously in the universal activity of unconditional blessing, we can finally realize, in our personal lives where it seems to matter the most, that there is no situation, no set of circumstances, no sequence of events in which Spirit is not holding constant blessing for us. Come what may in the outer arena of events and circumstances, Spirit is here, sourcing us, literally *sponsoring* us, helping us to learn to incarnate, yet more maturely than before, our share of what Spirit is.

Some situations don't feel good? No problem. We're not here to do life merely on the level of likes and dislikes anyhow. We're not here to do life on the level of getting our needs filled or playing favorites or attachments or endearments. Our true genius, our spark of divine wisdom, doesn't need all that. Our true genius does not need conditional agendas and reasons to bless what is going on in our lives or to find our next threshold of learning and growing. Our true genius knows how to go with the flow of what's happening in our lives, letting the experience of happiness grow not from playing the odds of need fulfillment or from playing likes and endearments against dislikes and judgments, but from grounding ever more deeply in our inner divine nature.

Challenge Happens

Our true genius is naturally curious about how we can express yet more of this divine nature in the incarnate world of time and space and circumstance—and so it is not surprised or thrown off when outer circumstances have a way of *testing* us.

Challenge happens. Our *relationship* with challenge is what matters. Our relationship with challenge is a crucial arena in which we can do our essential inner work and awaken our inner genius. Like all other relationships, our relationship with challenge can keep us learning how—

✧ Judgment weakens.
✧ Gratitude and blessing strengthen.
✧ We feel best, we feel most fit, when we get back to wholeness.[2]

As we expand our awareness and our aliveness beyond the weakening grip of judgment, we can fine-tune our relationship with challenge. We can learn to relate to challenge from the perspective that, after all, our greater good is always trying to come to us. And in fact our greater good is always succeeding in coming to us—our greater good

---

2 See Chapter 9, page 77.

is succeeding in coming to us precisely as much as we are *allowing* it to. Challenge tests our ability to allow.

Allowing is what enables us to see the movement of greater good into our lives as a *process*. Allowing enables us to stay present to whatever phase of the process we find ourselves in. As in any process, we can't expect later phases to unfold if we have been resisting being present to the current phase—and this is especially true when the current phase feels challenging.

Challenge tests our ability to keep allowing rather than resisting.

Challenge tests our ability to keep engaging life consciously and unconditionally.

The Rhythm of Awareness and Healing

There is a natural rhythm of awareness and healing that is meant to unfold in times of challenge. The more we can hold ourselves to this natural rhythm, the more we are likely to succeed in—

✧ Transcending judgment.
✧ Healing underlying layers of anger, hurt, weakness, etc.
✧ Staying true to love; and
✧ Living in wholeness, consciously allowing the sacred aliveness of the infinite whole to live in us, as us.

This rhythm flows in six stages. We are meant to see challenge as an invitation to—

1. Allow a simple, honest awareness of the situation. Keep it simple, just feel the feelings. If there's pain feel the pain, if there's confusion feel the confusion, if there's judgment

feel the judgment. Keep your awareness direct and present, without analyzing. Analyzing is likely to engage the rational or conditioned mind. Allowing yourself to simply and honestly *feel* the feelings, meanwhile, is an essential first step in *blessing* the whole situation.

2. Refresh your awareness in the simple truth that *now, as always, the activity of the living Spirit is present,* and that *the activity of Spirit is to generate love and blessing to support our growth.*

This stage is essential, simply because it refines our awareness. As we said earlier, in the chapter on Higher Mind, awareness always refines when it entertains the living truth of Spirit. You've probably been feeling this refinement as you read and reflect. What is essential here is that *as our awareness refines we can participate more freely in the activity of the One Mind or Higher Mind.* So as you refresh your awareness in the knowing that right here, right now, as always, Spirit is generating love and blessing to support your growth, let your awareness feel that it is opening and tuning to the workings of the Higher Mind.

3. Simply ask, How is this challenging situation prompting my further growth and learning? If I were to really bless this situation, would I start seeing it differently? How would I see it? What is it asking of me? How am I to respond? If my greater good is trying to come to me now, in this time of challenge, what would it come to me looking like? And how can I allow it in? What is it that *life* is asking of me? And what is being asked of my *relationship* with life, of how I

do life? How am I to find the real blessing in this challenge? (The exact formulation of your question will, of course, arise from the specific situation you're dealing with.)

The *next* stage is the big one, the stage in which real healing and resolution can start to unfold. If you sense that your awareness, your presence to the situation, is not quite ready for healing to really occur, you can always spend a little more time with the first three stages. (Remember, this whole process is a *rhythm* of awareness and healing. And once you're familiar with the rhythm of this you'll probably find that you don't even need to think in terms of six distinct stages—you'll just flow with the rhythm.) In any case, it is the first three stages of this rhythm that *tune our awareness,* and this is essential because it brings into play a simple but powerful principle, the principle that—

Awareness promotes healing.

Clear awareness of any challenge can flow quite readily into phases of very real, very effective healing—but only when the awareness is well-tuned.

4. As you tune in, intending that your inquiry lead to new understanding, resolution and healing, your "answer" will probably start to awaken as an energy event, a vital unfolding of energies responding to your awareness and to your intention. Keep tuning your awareness. Tune in to these energies.

These are the actual energies
that have been involved in your challenge,
as well as the energies that are
mobilizing for resolution and healing.

As you let your awareness engage these energies intuitively and fluidly, you are working in precisely the style of the Higher Mind. Entrust your process to this overarching spiritual intelligence. Having your next steps emerge can become remarkably easy as you entrust the process to the Higher Mind.

Go with what is unfolding. You may sense energetic sensations such as, for example, congestion or heaviness around your solar plexus. (This is just an example.) You may sense an intuitive knowing about what the sensation means, such as realizing, say, that your solar plexus is backlogging fear and uncertainty issues. You may sense further knowing about this, such as (again, these are examples) that your fear and uncertainty issues are being triggered by a recent new wrinkle in your life, perhaps the new shift supervisor at work. You may sense yet further knowing about it all, such as that you never quite cleared your old fear and uncertainty issues from an old conflict from your past. You see the pattern. Let these stages of understanding unfold. When the time is right—and this part is up to the Higher Presence—you will feel energies gathering to help you deal with what you are understanding, to help you shift, to help you start resolving and healing as much of your pattern as may be ready to shift. These energies are stirring from the infinite resourcefulness that is Spirit—and Spirit is evenly present in all things, including, of course, in every aspect of your challenge. It's not that the challenge has somehow separated you from the infinite resourcefulness of Spirit and that you need to "get rid" of the challenge in order to find your way back to Spirit. Radical as this may seem to the challenged mind, the universal spiritual activity of blessing can stir from within your challenged state and express as precisely those healing energies that can resolve the whole situation—if you but stay consciously present to the challenge with an attitude of blessing.

Consciousness completes the equation.

Happily, it is not up to us to generate the healing energy. Entrust that to Spirit. Stay present to the process—but don't try to make it happen. Relax in the knowing that, as we said earlier—

> *Awareness and intention always*
> *promote healing.*

I have seen this countless times. When we see a challenge clearly for what it is, it yields.

If your awareness is really tuned in you can literally observe this, or track it within your knowingness. Energetic problems and their underlying causes, such as the solar plexus congestion and the layered issues suggested in the example above, literally yield to the natural healing power of awareness and intention aligned to Spirit. As this occurs, your knowingness may pick up on specific currents or themes of healing energy, such as—

✧ A distinct movement of soul light into the contours of the situation, refreshing your ability to see the situation with more compassion and wisdom.

✧ Or perhaps a rallying of your innate, "gut" power, to restore and rebuild the energy state of your solar plexus.

✧ Or the play of insight and light showing you clearly how the outer circumstances of your challenge are reflecting a limiting or disempowering thought pattern within you, a thought pattern that is ready to yield to healing. (Recall Chapter 6: The physical world is just the outer arena of thought, reflecting back to us what's going on in the inner arena of thought, i.e., in our consciousness).

✧ Or a stirring of the divine power of release to break up your investment in judging your challenge. (It's so much easier for healing energies to mobilize within a challenge when we stop investing in judging the situation!)

✧ Or the play of healing energies to at least soften your judgment so you can see the deeper layers within the judgment—the anger, the hurt, the sadness, the neediness, the inadequacy, the fear, the separation wounds—and start clearing these deeper levels. (We usually carry a lot of charge within these layers, and this charge needs to process.)

✧ Or perhaps, if your inner work has prepared you for an elegant breakthrough, a stirring of the divine power of forgiveness and grace—a very real and tangible spiritual energy that can clear the old charge in a way that is, to our normal perspective, miraculous. (Though in the eyes of Spirit forgiveness, grace, and miracles are normal.)

✧ Or perhaps a quickening of your authentic happiness, your unconditional spiritual joy, to help you see that you've been giving your power to something outside yourself as if that external condition gets to determine your happiness.

✧ Or perhaps a refining of your true self-awareness to help you see that who you really are is not, after all, the troubled false self, or "I," that was feeling "I don't feel good" or "I don't like the new shift supervisor at work," etc.

✧ Or a rallying of your *amusement* about it all, one of the most freeing and, often, indispensable healing energies!

✧ Or a retrieval of your power from places along the timeline of your past where it had gotten lost. (This is a very common phenomenon).

✧ Or the play of insight and light that reminds you your real power is based on a God-given innocence that doesn't need to be proven in the face of challenge. (Would that we all retrieved this, our original power!)

✧ Or the *quickening* of your original power, re-empowering you to carry on in your original soul mission, the sacred mission to stay true to love. Love is the ultimate healing force. Most challenges cannot even co-exist with the healing vibration of pure love. And when we stay true to love, Spirit stays true to miracles, grace, and healing.

These are a few examples of what could unfold. With Spirit all things are possible. Blessing happens, healing happens.

How well our awareness *tracks* the healing is not really crucial. Often, we *are* able to track very specific energy currents, themes and insights, like those suggested above, and these can feel cogent and helpful, sometimes spectacularly helpful. Then again there may be times when we feel that we're not picking up on anything much more than a general sensation that our issue seems to be shifting or that our energy state seems to be upgrading. At such times a great deal of healing may be going on, even though we're not tracking it clearly. That can happen. Once the rhythm of awareness and healing is well underway, much can occur that is not tracked consciously.

At yet other times we may be tracking the play of insight and healing as it unfolds on one level while discerning, on a deeper level, what the deeper learning here is—

   ✧   The universal spiritual activity of blessing really
       is present in all moments and all circumstances.
   ✧   We serve this divine plan of universal blessing—
       and it serves us—when we welcome all experience,
       especially challenge, with an attitude of blessing.
   ✧   Judgment weakens, but blessing strengthens.
       Blessing keeps us spiritually fit and connected to
       the wholeness of universal sacred aliveness.

Go with what is happening for you. Keep it simple, keep entrusting the process to the Higher Presence. As each healing shift unfolds, align your intention to it—which is easy to do, since you're already in the energy of the shift.

As you align your intention, the healing shift carries.

Know that when healing shifts occur, the results in your life can be very profound. You will find yourself moving into exciting new thresholds of learning and growing, often unforeseen and way beyond what your rational or conditioned mind could have ever worked out. If you practice the rhythm of awareness and healing regularly and note what you're experiencing and learning, you could probably fill a journal easily with what you're learning and how you're growing.

Do practice often. In fact, many issues *require* multiple rounds of dedicated awareness and ever-more conscious healing.

Sometimes it helps to have a trusted friend support you, especially if your issues are really "up" at the time. Your friend can create a supportive space for you, "hold the energy," and coach you through the steps.

5. Practice gratitude. There's a lot to be grateful for here— greater insight, new healing, a deeper command of the rhythm of awareness and healing, plus the likelihood that all this will build and grow over time. We've cleared the way for more of our good to come to us, both now and over time.

   At every point in time, we receive most by being most open to receive. And gratitude is what keeps us most open to receive.

   The style of gratitude that serves best is unconditional gratitude. Throughout your process of awareness and healing, you've had a sponsor and an ally—the Higher Presence, the living Spirit. This is immensely significant. It means that, *aside* from gaining whatever specific insight and healing you may have gained—

Staying true and present to your process
of awareness and healing
has deepened your working relationship with Spirit.

This is always our greatest reward. It merits a style of gratitude that is unconditional, free of reasons and reasonings. A deeper relationship with Spirit is its own reward. Centering in unconditional gratitude fulfills the teaching to seek first the kingdom of Spirit—that is, to seek a deepening relationship with Spirit for the sake of Spirit, not for the sake of what we can get out of it.

Certainly there is a place for more conditional forms of gratitude as well—such as "I'm glad my solar plexus is feeling better, because now I can make a better impression on the new supervisor;" or "I'm thankful that I'm getting my power back from the relationship with so and so, because that relationship wasn't working and now I can use my power to attract a better relationship;" or "I'm grateful that I'm clear about my pattern of fatigue reflecting inadequacy feelings, because now I can get healthier"—but keep your perspective. The province of these more conditional forms of gratitude usually turns out to be the conditioned mind. Conditions and reasons for gratitude and blessing intrigue the conditioned mind. But will a feeling of gratitude that is based on specific limited conditions take us back into the experience of the sacred wholeness of life? Probably not. Will slipping into the more conditioned style of mind weaken or diffuse the whole rhythm of awareness and healing? Very possibly. Nonetheless, if we keep our perspective—that the real value of having our good come to us in life is that it reflects the infinite, unconditional good that lives in us, as us—then yes, conditional gratitude has a place. As we shall see in Chapter 16, conditioned mind and its conditional behaviors are not the real problem.

Our gratitude stays unconditional as we learn to "keep it simply sacred." If there was ever an area of life to keep simply sacred, it would be this whole area of how we handle challenges. Challenges can trigger layer upon layer of hurt feelings, wobbly communications, taking things too personally, blame games, win/lose thought patterns, attachment to outcome, contention and competition, investment in being right, fear of being wrong, plus the core fear triggered by all challenge, i.e. the fear of being separate from the sacred wholeness of life—*plus* all the backlogged charge we still carry from *past* times when we were triggered and didn't heal these layers. Times of challenge can get very complicated and messy.

How do we break that pattern? How do we bring it all back from complicated to simple, from messy to sacred? By centering in gratitude and blessing, and learning to let our gratitude and blessing be *unconditional*. All things truly of Spirit are unconditional. We learn to let Spirit live in us and inspire in us a simple, sacred approach to times of challenge. Then we discover that we can circumvent most of the drama, complication, and mess. *And* we find that our experience of healing is lifted to a level that is eminently effective, a level of directly *shifting the energy.*

Directly shifting the energy is usually the most successful approach to true healing.

The seasoned mind comes sooner or later to a kind of "clincher" or ultimate reason why we might as well keep it simple and sacred—

> *Most if not all of the challenges that*
> *show up in our lives are actually manifesting*
> *for no other reason than to keep us evolving*
> *our ability to bond with Source*
> *and to live from Source.*

In other words, were it not for the fact that staying true and present in times of challenge strengthens our ability to draw from Source, we would not be manifesting challenges! So we might as well keep it simple and bless them—"KISS"[3] them, if you will. Especially since the stream of challenges will not really end until we have gotten what we needed from them, until, that is, we have bonded quite totally with our divine Source.

What blocks total bonding is the core fear, the anguished dread deep in the psyche, that a life sourced totally from Spirit may not make us happy and fulfilled. This very fear

---

3 Keep it simply sacred.

keeps us in a thought paradigm in which we see ourselves and Spirit as separate. But—

> *All we really need to learn*
> *is that we are not separate from Source!*

To the seasoned mind that has seen that this is all the game of life is really about, challenges are welcome opportunities to deepen and strengthen our bond with Source, with the infinite Spirit. Challenges are times to let our co-creative dance with Spirit stay on course. Challenges are times to remember that we are destined to learn to live in life's most natural state—the state of authentic soul freedom and unconditional sacred aliveness—and to remember that we might as well let the learning be simple, easy and joyous.

6. Release. Entrust the outcome to divine order. Let go of attachment to any specific outcome.

Another way to say this is, by now there's nothing left to do but let the universe "add unto you" whatever outcome it can.

The exact outcome is always beyond our control. It takes the unlimited, ongoing computing capacity of the infinite Spirit to shape and direct what goes on in the outer world of time, space and circumstance, and this computing is way beyond our comprehension or control. But as we've seen in the previous chapter, the real value of any outcome is the *reflection* it adds, the reflection of the indwelling divine presence that lives in us, as us. This inner presence is what we are choosing to center in when we practice release.

If we have done the essential inner work of *owning* our indwelling divine nature, the reflections shall come.

Keep in mind that reflections occur, like everything else in this living universe, as quantum energy events. Reflections of our good, therefore, may be most available to us at subtle vibrational levels where the dance of energy interfaces with our consciousness. If so, we simply *feel the energy* of this and know that the universe is reflecting our good back to us as positive energy.

Sometimes the reflection materializes, as well, in the physical plane, looking like the specific outcome that we had in mind. In these cases we get to enjoy the reflection both energetically and materially

Then again, some reflections materialize looking quite *different* than the outcome we had in mind—in which case our whole growth spiral of *staying true to love by blessing all things unconditionally* may have to start taking another turn!

In every case, our role is to keep our consciousness well tuned, entrust the outcome to Spirit, and let go.

And be free.

Recap—The Rhythm of Awareness and Healing

1. Allow simple, honest awareness. Feel the feelings.

2. Refresh your awareness in the knowing that now as always Spirit is generating love and blessing to support your growth. As your awareness refines in this knowing, you can feel your awareness opening and tuning more to the activity of the Higher Mind.

3. Ask, How is this challenging situation prompting my further growth and learning? What is being asked of me? etc.

4. Allow your "answer" to unfold energetically as an energy event or events. As these occur they can convey greater understanding of the situation and, even more importantly, they will carry you into healing shifts.

5. Practice gratitude.

6. Release. Entrust the outcome to divine order. Let go of attachment to any specific outcome.

Chapter 11

The Ascendancy of the Sacred Feminine

There is perhaps no more freeing place than Mt. Shasta in which to explore the co-creative dance with Spirit. Whenever I lead a group to a power spot on this mountain I encourage each person to be totally open to new adventure. On one such occasion I led a group into a very special alpine meadow at 7,300 feet and encouraged each person to freely follow their instincts, commune with the meadow, tap into the energies there, explore, meditate, as their instincts may lead them. I myself did the same. After awhile I felt drawn to a spot along the little mountain spring where Janet, one of the group, had perched herself.

"Mark!" she exclaimed, "sit down, you gotta check out the energy here!" I sat down next to her. Janet guided my hands to hover, palms down, just above the earth at the edge of the spring. "Now feel the energy here!" she said. She was right, there was a noticeable pulse of energy right there, subtle, rhythmic, and distinctly nurturing. I let it wash into my senses. It felt sweet and loving, wonderfully nurturing, and distinctly feminine. "Bring it in all the way," coaxed Janet. I leaned closer to the earth. The energy pulse there was drawing me into a lovely sensation of safety and togetherness, the profound togetherness of all God's family, all sentient beings everywhere, united in love.

"It's the heartbeat of the Mother!" said Janet.

"Coming through beautifully," I said. I had to smile as I realized that we were sitting at precisely the same spot along the spring where, a couple of years earlier, members of *that* year's group had felt drawn to tune in to the sacred feminine energies of Spirit. "This spot draws many," I said. "It's like a portal here."

We lingered for a while, pleasuring in the energy arousal we were feeling and appreciating the signature love of the sacred feminine presence, the sense of tender assurance that every life-form, every spark of new life issuing from the divine Godhead, shall be lovingly cared for, evolved, and carried back home, back into the sacred wholeness of Spirit.

So began an extraordinary day of workshopping with the sacred feminine aspect of God, the Divine Mother.

The Sacred Feminine

Soon it was time for the group to gather. We met in a natural circle of rocks and trees a short distance from the spring. I opened with a little invocation to "set the energy," a simple practice I always do before a workshop segment to tune in and give voice to the higher-dimensional energy states and energy blessings that are ripening for the group in the moment—and this time, not surprisingly, it was all about the Sacred Feminine.

Like all things, Spirit displays two complementary aspects, a masculine aspect and a feminine aspect, much like the universal polarity that is often described as the polarity of yin and yang. Within the realm of Spirit there is—

✧ A masculine aspect, which *expresses* divinity; and

✧ A feminine aspect, which *embodies* divinity.

Said another way—

✧ The Father principle *creates* form; and

✧ The Mother principle *nurtures* form.

The Father is the creative principle—the Father creates the infinite potentials of life and sets them into motion. The Mother is the nurturing principle—nurturing the infinite potentials of life into the highest embodiment of divine nature that they can blossom into.

Of course these two aspects of the Godhead are ultimately not two but one, as Spirit is transcendently unitary. But in our times the Sacred Feminine aspect of God is "on the move" and rising in the awakening consciousness of the times as She emerges—or re-emerges, having long been repressed—as an absolutely key element of our journey back to wholeness. As the Sacred Feminine awakens in human consciousness and human culture She re-kindles the values of nurturance, respect, accountability, tenderness, interconnectedness and holism so desperately needed to balance and bless human activity and ensure that what we create serves life and honors life. This is the passion of the Mother, to champion life, to see that life is served and honored. Like a mother raises her child to reach its full potential, Divine Mother is "raising the universe" to evolve to its highest expression of divine potentials.

"Blessed All That Be"

I always love it when individuals share their experience in a workshop, because as they speak they transmit the energy of their experience, enriching all of us. That day on the mountain, it was time for Janet to share.

"I was sitting there, and I started to go into meditation," she began, "and I felt the most powerful *heartbeat* coming at me from the earth, and I felt like I was swaying with it and then I was in unison with it...it was going...pulse...pulse...I still feel it as I talk about it, it almost takes your breath away. And I got into the rhythm of it and I was told to run it up through all of my chakras and to take it up all the way, and that with each beat was coming knowledge of the divine, knowledge of the earth, knowledge of exquisite love, knowledge that this is available for all. What a buzz, I still feel it!

"It's like *the purest essence of healing.* Completely pure. And when it comes in it goes into your DNA, that's what it feels like, every little cell is going Yeah! It feels *so good* and the sense is that you are so connected and not alone. And no matter what has happened, no matter what you've been through, this is available to *everyone* because that is what the Divine Mother wants. Nobody is alone. You *can't* be alone. You can't be in trouble. She's completely nonjudgmental. It's the unconditional love of the universe. She loves completely, purely. It's all-encompassing. It takes your breath away!"

Janet's enthusiasm was building and emanating into all of us. "Go to your heart and you can feel it," she encouraged us, "I know you can feel it. She *loves* that inner child in all of us. She wants you to feel this—*you are a being of grace."* Janet's voice rang with conviction. "And you *belong* to Her. And you belong to *each other."*

As Janet's enthusiasm reached its peak she found words that, I believe, capture brilliantly the real essence of the Divine Mother's love—

"Blessed all that be!"

That's it! That is the essence and that is what we are all called to learn—in the love of the Mother, all that be are exquisitely blessed.

In the eyes of the Mother we are all one family, and in the love of the Mother we are all completely enfolded and blessed.

"One-derful"

When the love of Divine Mother comes in it restores everything to oneness. That is why it is "the purest essence of healing." In oneness there can be no sense of trouble, for all trouble originates in the belief in separation. When the Divine Mother comes along with her sovereign assurance, *"You belong to Me, you belong to each other, you are not separate, we are one,"* all sense of separation and trouble within us yields. All sense of separation and trouble is vibrationally lifted and transformed, for—

- ✧ Oneness is the ultimate reality, and
- ✧ The experience of oneness is the ultimate healing.

One day, deep in meditation with the Sacred Feminine, I received the message, "The greatest bliss is the bliss of oneness." The truth of this has suffused itself like a mantle of certainty into my whole sense of a higher destiny. Fulfillment may be found on many levels, happiness may be found in many octaves, but the greatest bliss is the bliss of oneness. The assurance of this resonates in the heart of each of us, and Divine Mother will not rest until we all experience the bliss of oneness. *She will not rest.* On a personal scale, within the heart of each of us, and on an epic scale, within the cosmic fabric of the universe itself, the ascendancy of the Mother, of the universal Sacred Feminine, is quickening our deepest inner sense of sacred oneness and championing, just as swiftly as we can have it, our destined journey back into bliss.

Shrines

That day at Mt. Shasta we were swept powerfully into oneness. We were carried to the heightened plane of consciousness where we directly see that—

- ✧ All things enshrine the One, the living Spirit.
- ✧ The living Spirit in its Sacred Feminine aspect indwells all things and configures all things or literally matrixes them ("matrix" comes from the Latin *mater* for "mother") as shrines of the living Spirit. No part of creation can possibly be left out, every little bit of creation is organically matrixed into the One, into this sacred, living fabric of wholeness.

From this, our next stage of awakening sprang naturally—

- ✧ Each and every one of us enshrines the One, the living Spirit, and is lovingly called, by the grace of the Divine Mother, to awaken into our natural "shrine-hood."

We did. We became conscious shrines of the living Spirit. We saw ourselves as individual points in the universal weave of sacred aliveness, like nodes of light and love in a cosmic tapestry of light and love.

Shrine-Hopping

Spiritual workshopping always unfolds on many levels as the consciousness of the group responds to new thresholds of awareness, new currents of energy, new opportunities to learn and grow. To me the real alchemy that draws people into the workshop experience, as opposed to seeking awakening through other avenues such as reading, meditation, or working with CDs and other tools, is the opportunity to explore, in a heightened way, what it's like to—

✧ Incarnate our divinity passionately and well, and

✧ Have our divinity reflected to us, passionately and well, by the others in the workshop group, even as we reflect the same sacred essence to them.

It is simply unforgettable to do this. It is healing and life-transforming at a level that goes far beyond words.

As the group at Mt. Shasta was swept into conscious oneness we became extraordinarily fit to do this, to gift each other with reflections of our incarnate divinity. So began an inspired time of "shrine-hopping," of communing deeply, one-on-one, with each person in the group as a child of the One. It was poignant and playful, exhilarating and freeing, to come fully present to each person, shining our light, unfolding our love, coming alive in the sacred act of blessing.

That's the Spirit!

As we blessed each other we discovered the incredible passion of the Divine Mother. We discovered that—

When we open to bless another person,
the Divine Mother moves into the act.
Divine Mother pours her nurturing love into the act of blessing.

This means that as we bless, we become instruments of the Mother. And so we are invigorated by the Mother, we are vibrationally lifted to higher and higher frequencies of *shakti,* higher and higher octaves of the Mother's passion for life to blossom and evolve.

Passion is contagious. It spreads, if we let it, into all our relationships. And then the whole dynamic or "give and take" of our relationships can take on an even richer dimension of incarnating our divinity passionately and well. Then, quite literally, when we feel flushed and uplifted in the expanded state of sharing and giving, *that's the Spirit!* Literally, that's the living Spirit—that's the power and the passion of Spirit in its Sacred Feminine aspect, nurturing life and growing life from deep, deep within us.

Sacred Loop of Giving

Love only grows. The more of it you give, the more of it you have. The more love we give to each other, the more love we receive from our common Source. This synergistic principle of love can be formulated in many ways. That day at Mt. Shasta, we came to see the synergy of love as the province of the Sacred Feminine and the promise, literally, of the Sacred Feminine.

We can find this promise, and its fulfillment, in every new moment. It is the very signature of the Mother's presence. We are promised that—

As we give to life, life gives back to us.

Life subsists in a sacred loop of giving. And Divine Mother is right there, in the loop, in the synergy, overseeing it, working it, abiding by her promise. She thrills at each new act of giving, and ensures that life gives back. It is her passion. *Life must evolve.*

This makes the practice of kindness, generosity, compassion, and respect eminently sensible. This makes staying true to love eminently *sane*, to use the word from *A Course in Miracles*. We become sane at last as we realize that, no matter how much we may think we succeed in taking, we will not be nurtured, our soul will not be fed by what we take, if in the act of taking we have slighted the promise of the Sacred Feminine, if we have slighted the sacred alchemy of giving.

The Mother's promise stands—

> *As we give to life, life gives back to us.*
> *The surest way to evolve*
> *is with respect, kindness, generosity, and compassion.*

Chapter 12

Grounding and Presence

When the Sacred Feminine expresses to nurture life in our third-dimensional world of earth, air, water, cells, minerals, molecules, bodies, etc., we call her Mother Nature. And Mother Nature is a master in the ways of synergy. She is adept in bringing energies together with enough creativity, intelligence, and, most of all, harmony, to create whole new possibilities, often remarkable and unforeseeable.[4]

Mother Nature has found an ingenious way to design the synergy of giving—as we give to life, life always gives back—into how we function in this third-dimensional world. She has provided each of us with a fundamental instinct for staying in the loop. This instinct is *grounding*. As we shall see, the synergy, the sacred loop of giving, works like this—

⋄ We give to life the gift of our grounded presence and respect.
⋄ Life gives back to us the gift of essential support energies and nurturing energies.

---

4 Much gratitude goes to R. Buckminster Fuller for coining the term *synergy* for this phenomenon, back in the 1960s.

Grounding

It begins with grounding, a simple enough process, yet one with profound effects on how energies configure in our world.

Here is an easy and effective way to get started—

> Tune your awareness to the energy at the base of your
> spine. Let your awareness tune in to the energy center or
> chakra—the base chakra—at the very base of your spine.[5]
> This chakra is one of the most important energy centers
> Mother Nature has given us for managing our energies
> and, really, for managing our whole experience of incar-
> nating. To incarnate the living Spirit into earthly embodi-
> ment we need a system of energy centers to manage the
> process. Our chakras constitute such a system, anchoring
> higher dimensional light into the subtle energy bodies and
> the physical body, owning this light, and directing this
> light, or life-force, into all the functions of our bodies.[6]
>
> Tune your awareness to your base chakra, and see this
> chakra as alive with light.
>
> Next, see the very center of planet earth as alive with
> light. In fact some of the best light that can be found any-
> where in the universe is at the center of our own planet.
>
> Now you are aware of two distinct points of light—
> your base chakra and the center of the earth. Next, simply
> "connect the dots." See a natural movement of light con-
> necting your base to the center of the planet.
>
> That's it—just this easily, you're grounded.

---

5 If you're not sure whether you know how to tune in you can always just visualize.
Visualizing works. With a little more experience, what started out as visualizing feels just
like tuning in—and in fact it is.

6 As basic material about the chakras is familiar to most readers, we won't elaborate
it here.

The design of nature is that the base chakra *wants* to ground to the center of the earth, and the center of the earth *is meant* to attract and draw our grounding instinct to it. That is why the practice of grounding can occur very easily and naturally. The simple image given here, the image of connecting two points of light, seems to serve this ease and naturalness particularly well.

> Next, give yourself permission to consciously work with your grounding. Start by checking the width of the line of energy or stream of light or "grounding cord," as it's commonly called, that connects you to the earth. How wide is it? Commonly, people visualize it as more or less the width of a cord or a rope, but it can certainly be wider. Try making it as wide as your body. Feel how, as you do this, your whole body is more fully invited to participate in the feeling of being grounded. Now make it as wide as your energy field, feeling how your whole energy field or aura is being invited to more fully participate in the state of being grounded. Throughout your space, from your core chakra through all your other chakras, through your whole body and your whole energy field, let yourself feel powerfully drawn and grounded to the very center of the earth.

Conscious grounding in this way creates a tangible feeling of stability, a feeling of being safe and secure here on the earth plane.

This stability, in turn, draws us more fully into our bodies and helps us to feel more *present.* As we shall see, presence is the key to incarnating the living Spirit. *Presence is the key to coming alive unconditionally, to letting Spirit live in us, as us.*

Again, give yourself permission to work consciously with your grounding. As you tune in to the play of light, the activity of light, that connects you to the earth and stabilizes your presence on the earth, you may start to notice energy patterns here and there within your space that seem—relative to the play of light you're feeling—rather dense, or heavy, or dark, or clunky. These are energy blocks. These are patterns that are trying to run on something other than spiritual principle or spiritual truth. These are places where your energy got stressed or even stuck trying to invest in patterns that look away from spiritual principle, patterns such as—

- ✧ Judgment.
- ✧ Feelings of being separate, on your own, in trouble— and all the woundedness that develops from feeling separate, woundedness patterns such as fear, inadequacy, and anger.
- ✧ Conditional agendas, conditional beliefs, and investment in conditional happiness.
- ✧ Consensus that the world is a place of separation, limitation, conflict, fear, and loss.
- ✧ "Negative" input from the world reflecting the belief that life is about separation, limitation, conflict, fear, and loss.
- ✧ Stress accretion from all of this.

These patterns create clutter and noise and a certain density or weightedness in our space. They also tend to make us feel even more separate, more on our own. The grounding instinct is about *letting go* of all this, letting go of whatever does not participate in spiritual principle, letting go, especially, of whatever does not participate in the spiritual principle that—

All things are interconnected.

Grounding is about letting go of our separation wounds and seeking re-connection with something greater than ourselves. Grounding is about re-connecting with the sacred matrix of life.

As we have seen elsewhere in this book, letting go works out best when we let it be easy. Letting go of our energy blocks can be extraordinarily easy when we're well grounded—simply because these blocks do not participate in spiritual principle or spiritual truth and hence have a certain dead weight. Only truth is vibrationally pure. Everything else is, vibrationally speaking, cluttered or impure. Everything else is weighted. Only the truth endures, while everything else must pass away. In Sanskrit the word for "truth" literally means "that which endures." Grounding is our instinctual way to get back to what is true and real and enduring.

All energy blocks must fall away,
by their own dead weight,
and conscious grounding is the most natural way
to facilitate their release.

These blocks have taken time to build up in us, and it usually takes consistent release, over time, to clear them. Conscious grounding is not the only way to release them, of course, but it is the most foundational way. Over time, the habit of regular, conscious grounding supports, like nothing else can, our ongoing efforts to release the charge in our patterns of woundedness, stuckness, and stress.

Without the habit of conscious grounding, our wounds and blocks—because they are weighted—create a very real "drag" effect on our movement through time. They scatter our awareness. They can cause parts of our awareness to get stuck in the past, literally. As this occurs we feel less whole and alive. We feel less present.

But grounding is about re-connecting to wholeness. Grounding is about presence.

Refresh your grounding. See the light at the base of your spine, see the light at the center of the earth, connect the dots—and do this in present time, in the free and clear present moment.

Feel the natural gravitational pull of the earth that can draw to it, now, whatever is weighted. Notice the mass, the heaviness in your unresolved thoughts and feelings about the past. They're weighted, so let them drop into your grounding. Notice the weightedness in your worries about the future. Drop them too. Intend and have that all weighted energies in your space are dropping out of your space now, falling by their own density into the current of living light you've got running to the gravitational center of the earth. Let this intention carry for *all* the weighted energies in your space that can be released now, whether you're aware of them or not—and whether, for that matter, they are your own energies or just energies that you probably picked up from other people.

Know that as these denser energies reach the center of the earth they are transmuted by the light there, that Mother Nature has it set up that way.

See yourself as re-connected to the living truth that—

Life is now,

that there is only the Now, the eternal present. See your-self as re-stabilized in the sacred aliveness of the present moment. See yourself as free of the clutter and stress of the past, no matter how much that stress was pressing upon you a moment ago. See yourself as free of the uncer-tainties of the future too. Let yourself feel completely free to participate in unconditional sacred aliveness and living truth, *in this present moment.*

Presence Is Now

Spiritual freedom is a radical state. When we are truly free—when we are free in the living Spirit—anything at all that does not serve our ability to experience unconditional sacred aliveness and living truth, *in the present moment,* simply falls away.

Conscious grounding helps awaken this radical freedom. Con-scious grounding develops the habit of presence, grounded presence, and opens us into the authentic freedom of each new moment. As we refine this skill we start to feel that *grounding* and *being present* are becoming much the same thing, and that what we are grounding *to,* what we are being present *to,* is, simply, the natural state of freedom that the living Spirit endows into each and every moment.

Do it this way now. Refresh your grounding. See the light at the base of your spine, see the light at the center of the earth, connect the dots, doing all this in present time, in the free and clear present moment, knowing that what you are really re-connecting to is the spiritual state of freedom in the moment, in the eternal Now, which alone is real. Knowing that whatever is not serving your unconditional sacred aliveness, your highest good, in the free and clear present moment, is passing out of your reality and is past. What remains is the present. Be present.

Be presence itself.

Completing the Loop

Conscious grounding is a way of saying, "I want to allow life, not resist life. I want to keep myself free and present to the play of living truth. I am willing to stay connected, to be a part of the whole. I want to stop investing in feeling separate and troubled. I want to let the divine order of things have a chance to prevail. I want to keep evolving. And may life itself have every chance to keep evolving, through me and through all things. I will not withhold. Far be it for me to withhold myself from the processes of life. I want to be unconditionally alive. I know that a sacred life-force is expressing in me, as my life-force, and so I give my presence and my respect and my trust to the experience of life."

This is a huge gift—a gift to life. It is a way of upholding and affirming the sacred loop of giving that life subsists in. It makes us valuable to life and valuable to the Sacred Feminine, who oversees the synergy and ensures that life gives back to us. So—

- ✧ We give to life the gift of our grounded presence and respect.
- ✧ Life gives back to us the gift of essential support energies and nurturing energies.

Earth Energy, Support, and Nurturing

Life gives us this support and nurturing in many ways. First and foremost, life gives us a direct flow of supportive, nurturing energies from the same Mother Earth or Mother Nature that we have been grounding to. It's a very nice arrangement. The more we ground, the more we open to receive from the earth. And by "nature" or "earth" we mean *all* of nature, all the elements, the waters, the air, the fire, all the kingdoms, all the energy planes, the core of light, all that is woven into the phenomenon of existence on this planet, and, preeminently, the indwelling Spirit itself, that lives in this matrix of life as its very essence. We're talking about a profound matrix of incarnate life here, something that is not to be taken for granted. It is meant to grow us and sustain us in its energies. We discover, as we learn to tune to these energies and incorporate them into the dance of our individual lives, how deeply supportive, nurturing, calming, centering, and invigorating they really are.

Tune in once again. Refresh your grounding, feel your natural connectedness to the earth. As usual, give yourself permission to let go of anything in your space that is weighted or restricts your freedom in the moment. As you let go of weighted energies, feel yourself opening to receive new energies, energies of support from the earth.

You might imagine a gentle spring of underground energy that has been gathering and swelling within the earth and now starts to gently murmur and bubble and flow into the space of your being. You might imagine a pulse of love coming to you from the Earth Mother. You might imagine primal tones and earth resonances gently sounding in the earth, building and flowing and restoring you to the core wholeness and sacred aliveness of the planet.

You might imagine a fountain of life-force beneath you that lifts you into heightened awareness and presence. You might imagine a womb of great beauty and mystery, the mystery of life itself, enfolding you now in its sublime peace.

Take some time to commune with the gifts of the Earth.

It's a very satisfying experience to open to earth energies and to let them flow into us. Earth energies flow into us at the feet, at the legs, at the lower chakras, and are especially supportive there, in the "lower body," where our groundedness is fundamentally important. The energy of the earth is uniquely supportive, there's nothing quite like it. It supplies the lower body with an essential tone of stability and comfort, security, and safety. We all need to feel this fundamental support.

Earth energy supports us unconditionally.

Earth energy doesn't have any agendas, and it isn't about supporting our agendas either. Earth energy just supports life, incarnate life, here in the incarnate plane, the earth plane. Earth energy is not a powerful energy in the sense of being dramatic or galvanizing or enlightening or the power surge within a huge breakthrough or that sort of thing—but it is steady, and true, and abiding. It is always there for us. Earth energy is literally essential to our life here. It is meant to be part of the equation, part of the mix of energies that we work with. In fact if we did not want to work with earth energy we would not have chosen to incarnate here on earth—there are certainly other places in this multi-dimensional universe to spend time. But we did incarnate here. It takes a lot of support to be here and, happily, the energies of the earth provide fundamental support.

Draw the earth energy into you now. Tune in. Feel how your whole lower body resonates and responds and *welcomes* the abiding support of the earth. Ground to the earth. Commune with the earth. As the gifts of the earth build and grow within you they naturally flow more and more fully into the whole space of your being, supplying your entire body/mind/chakra system with peace, healing, and balance. Let this build. Let this carry you into *authentic presence.* You are a child of the Infinite, a divine soul, and you have chosen to incarnate here on planet earth, as a child of the earth. *Be* a child of the earth. Let yourself feel present as all incarnate beings are meant to feel present—centered, sentient, whole, content. *Grounded. In* your body. *In* the moment. *In* your wholeness and love. *In* your freedom and sacred aliveness. All these elements come together when you are present. *Be* truly present, be unconditionally here, unconditionally alive. Let your conditioned mind yield, let the resonant truth grow strong and clear—

> *Incarnate life is naturally whole.*
> *Incarnate life is naturally sacred.*

Commune with the sacred matrix of incarnate life, commune with the Mother Earth. Draw her to you. Receive her love.

Complete the loop.

Presence Versus Withholding

As we develop this skill of grounded, unconditional presence we train ourselves to honor life's fundamental synergy—

Presence supports life.
Life supports presence.

We train our energy state, and how we manage our energies. As we develop the skill of grounded, unconditional presence, we are learning to honor life's fundamental synergy by the whole way in which we manage our soul's experience of incarnating. As we said in chapter 9, incarnating divinity is the essential dharma or sacred duty that we are all called to, so how we *manage* the experience of incarnating is very important.

Cosmic Election

Imagine a cosmic election is underway. Imagine that every individual is asked to vote for one or the other of two simple proposals. One proposal calls for life in wholeness, interconnectedness and joy. This proposal is sponsored by the divine plan and set forth in spiritual principle. The other proposal calls for life in separation, conflict and fear. This proposal has no official sponsor, but seems to have arisen as a widespread alternative view set forth in mass consciousness consensus trends.

In this election, which is open and ongoing—

The "ballot" is the quantum world itself.

The ballot is precisely this world we live in, this living plasma of responsive energy that is imprinted and directed by what goes on in the consciousness of the people.

Every time an individual practices authentic, unconditional presence and respect, the ballot registers a vote for life in wholeness, interconnectedness and joy. These votes honor the essential dharma of incarnate life, and they sound a note of support. But every time an individual practices withholding, the ballot registers a vote for life in separation, conflict, fear and discord.

All these votes are tallied and reckoned on an ongoing basis and reflected or fed back into the consciousness of the people—*as the actual state of the world we live in.* This way, no one need wonder how the vote is going. No one need puzzle about how their consciousness habits are affecting the outer world. The actual state of the world provides clear and direct demonstration.

This continuous feedbacking is meant to assist us. It is meant to draw us into ever more conscious, responsible presence. It is meant to draw us into ever more fit and well-tuned participation in the whole synergistic loop of presence and support that our lives in this incarnate world are meant to be.

And the stakes are high.

Withholding

Let us examine what is at stake. When an individual practices withholding rather than grounded presence, their "vote" implicitly weakens both themselves and the fabric of life as a whole. They are voting for resisting life, not allowing life. They are saying, "I don't want to stay free and present to the play of living truth. I don't want to stay connected, to be a part of the whole." They are choosing to hold on to their issues rather than release them, and to decline any notion of a higher order, a higher intelligence, a divine plan that can work things out on a higher level of spiritual principle. In effect, they are taking it upon themselves to strategize their lives on their own, to impose their personal agendas, beliefs, or conditions on what is going on.

They may be strategizing, for example, that by holding on to their issues they can—

✧ Control what is going on, in order to wrest what they want from the situation. (Control, it seems, becomes the instinctual comfort zone of the conditioned psyche.)

✧ Hide their issues, their pain, etc. so that other people won't see the issues and won't be aware of the pain.

✧ Hide their issues from themselves, so that they themselves won't have to reckon with the issues, feel the pain, etc.

✧ Let other people get a glimpse of their issues, but use this to manipulate people.

✧ Let other people get a glimpse of their issues, but use this as a reason to not open up and show people what they fear is the real person, for fear that if others saw this supposed real person they would judge it.

You see the pattern. Withholding gets devious. What may have started as a simple and seemingly innocent feeling of distrust, for whatever reason, can easily start playing out as divisive behaviors like control, manipulation, deception, and judgment—behaviors that have stalled and confounded, for far too long, all our efforts to become genuinely, unconditionally present to each other in conscious wholeness.

Withholding votes against wholeness. Withholding opposes the sacred synergy of giving.

The person who withholds is, most of all, withholding their true self, their divine soul. And this is very weakening. This can become tragic—

The divine soul nature is literally
less able to incarnate, less able to be there
ensouling the consciousness of the person who withholds.

When soul-to-body coordination declines, feelings of separation can grow even more real and compelling, as can all the separation wounds, the fear, the anger, the judgment, etc. When soul-to-body coordination declines, so does the felt level of real wisdom, resourcefulness, and adaptability—which means the issues that triggered the whole withholding process suffer less and less likelihood of finding true resolution. The sense of separation may become so ingrained that it feels natural and acceptable. In our culture, for centuries, the prevailing paradigm would suggest that being separate and on one's own is in fact how to be present, that being separate and on one's own is what existential human presence really comes down to, that it is somehow noble or ennobling to stand one's ground as a separate being—when in truth this condition is anything but authentic presence! It is chronic withholding. It leaves the individual disconnected from the sacred wholeness of life and it leaves the rest of us *missing* him or her. We all came to earth on a soul mission to explore the creative, synergistic, transformational power of divine love, and we need each other to *be here*, soulfully present, coming from love, getting on with why we're here. Until this happens a deep and sorrowed confusion will continue to trouble the collective consciousness of the human family.

Energy Has to Move

There is more to the drama. Issues are *energy.* As issues arise, our moment to moment choices or "votes" for either presence or separation set themes and conditions on how energy can flow and configure in our world.

Issues are energy
and energy has to move.

Energy can't do nothing. Even if we try to invoke extreme separation and withholding, the energy in our issues has to move. The energy may try to obey the paradigm of separation and withholding by seeking to calcify or turn numb, but this effect will be provisional at best, for in the processes of life there is no true numbness. There is only withholding versus trusting. Or as we said it in chapter 1, the only real choice is between—

Resisting life versus allowing life.

In all possible scenarios, there is one reality—life. And life is alive with energy.

Awareness and Healing

When we are feeling the energy of our issues and we know this energy has to move, we always have choices. Usually the key is awareness— how much awareness are we maintaining in the midst of the issues? *If awareness is clear and present in present time it will tend to move in natural healing directions.* This is true regardless of whether the individual has studied metaphysical principles. *Anyone* who is present and clear can find themselves moving naturally in the direction of—

✧ *Grounding.* It is natural to feel a connectedness to the earth we all live on and to let the excess charge in our issues ground or discharge to the earth. It is natural to draw new support and strength from the earth.

✧ *The rhythm of awareness and healing,* as described in chapter 10. It is natural to ask, "What is the real lesson in my issues, what is being asked of me here?" and to stay present to the healing energy shifts and insights that are wanting to emerge from our felt issues.

These natural healing instincts always help. But sometimes, just because our issues are really "up," we may not feel as tuned in or as inclined to use these forms of energy resolution, or to work them really successfully. Sometimes we may resort to the most basic healing instinct of all—

✧ *Talking about it.* We make the choice to communicate about our issues, either to a trusted friend, or to the person with whom we are feeling the issues (if possible and if appropriate), or even to the night sky or to the breeze or to the cat or to our journal.

The point of talking about it is that we give the energy a chance to move. Conscious communication can be spectacularly successful. The energy moves and clears, and we feel much better. Afterwards we usually feel like we've learned all over again the remarkable healing power of just letting it out, of *talking about it.*

But sometimes conscious communication isn't enough. Sometimes, after we've done our best on the level of conscious communication, our issues still feel charged with unresolved energy. And there are other times when conscious communication is not an option anyhow. Sometimes, for example, it's simply not possible or not practical to communicate with the person with whom we are feeling issues. A good example is that it's not necessarily a good idea to tell our employer, the person who controls our paycheck, exactly how we're feeling about them. Or maybe for one reason or another the timing is unfavorable and we have to mark time for awhile. In cases like this we always have another option, an eminently healthy way to let the energy in our issues have a chance to move and resolve. We can communicate *on a higher level,* on a level that I have learned to call *superconscious.*

Superconscious Communication

We all have a superconscious self, an aspect of our divine soul nature that functions on higher planes to give shape and direction to the flow of our conscious lives. This superconscious self commands a heightened perspective on our lives. It directly sees that our goodness and our worthiness are always in place, that our goodness and our worthiness are in fact God-given and quite absolute. It sees beyond any limits of conventional time and space. It sees how the divine plan, the play of living truth, and all the unlimited resources of the higher planes can be tapped and enlisted to give new shape and direction to our conscious lives according to our readiness. And it sees how all of us, on a superconscious level, are interconnected.

Communicating on this level can be incomparably effective. Many a student and client have told me "I wish I had thought of this before!"

and I felt that way myself when I first sorted out how communicating on a superconscious level works. Simply—

1. Tune in to this higher aspect of your true self, who knows impeccably well that—

    ❖ Your goodness and your worthiness are absolute and God-given.
    ❖ You are not limited in time and space.
    ❖ The same is true for everyone else, as we are all equal and interconnected.

2. Summon the corresponding, superconscious level of the person you want to work with. On this superconscious level, the other person always hears. Welcome their response, welcome that you and them are connected.

3. *Appreciate* the other person on this level. *Love* them—everyone is very beautiful on this level! So let them know you see their beauty. Be genuine of course. But know that this little moment of communion, as a prelude to communication, is often enough to promote some very real healing and resolution.

4. Address the particular issues you've been feeling. Communicate what needs to be communicated. Speak (either silently or aloud) with conviction, centering your conviction in the simple knowing that—

    ❖ Your superconscious self speaks from higher truth and with the natural authority to command highest good for your life.

✧   The superconscious self of the other person hears you in higher truth and with a natural respect for the highest good.

As you speak from truth the right words flow, cogently and compassionately, because *the truth is alive and self-directing*. The truth knows what needs to be said and how to say it.

5.   Release your communication with trust. Relax. Be sure to return to your normal state of being grounded and present, in the body, in present time.

You may want to ask a trusted friend to support you in this work, especially if your issues are really "up" at the time. Your friend can create a supportive space for you, "hold the energy," and coach you through the steps.

Here is an example of superconscious communication:

Martha is upset with her elderly mother Eunice for acting like a victim. Eunice always says, in so many words, "Why should I try, I'm just a hopeless old lady" whenever Martha tries to get Eunice more involved in constructive activities at her assisted living home. Eunice's listlessness is wearing on Martha. And Martha doesn't like it that she has to play into her mother's pattern just to be nice and not make waves. Martha is vexed that the whole relationship, the quality of time that she and Eunice spend together, is becoming depressed. Efforts at discussing this with her mother have not helped much.

So Martha realizes that it's time to give the issue over to a higher level. She may think of it as, "I'm going to have a talk with Mom, soul to soul." She composes herself, perhaps goes into meditation, and calls in the superconscious connection. She speaks lovingly to her mother, "Mom, I love you so much. You are so beautiful. I love it that you are in my life. I want you to know that I see the real you, the strong vibrant Eunice as God made you. I know that you can create your reality. I know that you can shift your attitude, maybe more than you know, and start to feel more interested in life again. That's the real you, Mom. Go for it, please! I need you to know that I am not willing to go along with your hopelessness role as if it's fine. I am not available for that. I believe in the real you!" As Martha communicates she realizes there's more to the story—"and Mom, I am not willing to feel guilty because you're in assisted living now. You know it was the best decision. You know you're best provided for there. You know I would do *anything* for you if it's really for the best. But I am not willing to feel guilty on your behalf. Mom, if your depressed behavior is meant to make me feel guilty, it won't work. I love you so much! Let's be happy when we're together! We still have so much beauty and joy to share with each other. I believe in the real you, and I won't stop believing, I won't stop knowing what I know. And I know that you hear me too. Thank you for hearing me, and thank you for responding to me on this level of truth. I look forward to happy times with you!"

As Martha speaks she feels a new calmness and conviction. It's clear that the charge in her issues has largely resolved. In the ensuing days Martha's visits to her mother reveal a real shift in Eunice, new light in her eyes, new pep in her voice, a new interest in enjoying her life and, most of all, a new closeness to Martha.

Stories like this have become commonplace in my work. I have seen the superconscious approach work extraordinarily well. The person initiating the superconscious communication feels new currents of healing and resolution, and, while the communication itself has occurred on a higher or superconscious level, the conscious behavior of the other person shows that they "got it" too.

It's all about energy. Issues are energy, and energy has to move. It's very instructive and freeing sometimes to see our world as an energy world, and to appreciate that we are all energy beings sharing a common energy world. The more we see things from this point of view, the more we get it about how deeply interconnected we really are.

Prayer

If superconscious communication moves energy and resolves issues by lifting the whole matter to a superconscious level, effective prayer takes things even further. Prayer can be seen as a variation on superconscious communication and an expansion of superconscious communication. Like superconscious communication, prayer must start with tuning in. We tune in to the higher or superconscious part of ourselves and to our certainty about our goodness and our worthiness and our access to the resources of this multi-dimensional universe. Then, we send our communication. This time, we make the communication more open-ended. This time—

*We intend that our communication
reach the divine intelligence of the universe as a whole,
not just this intelligence as it lives in another person.*

Issues Find Healing as We Stay Present

Issues are not really problems. They are, as we saw in chapter 10, opportunities to grow by strengthening our working relationship with spiritual principle and our ultimate oneness with the infinite Spirit. We always have at least five healthy options for approaching issues in this way and for helping the energy in them to move—

✧ Grounding.
✧ The rhythm of awareness and healing (Chapter 10).
✧ Conscious communication.
✧ Superconscious communication.
✧ Prayer.

Each of these approaches fosters a natural movement of energy toward resolution, insight and healing. Each of these approaches "votes" for life in wholeness, interconnectedness and joy. And each of these approaches relies on our simple *presence*, our genuine, trusting, respecting *presence*.

Default

But when an individual *withholds* their presence, they tend to not be very open to these healing options, or even aware of them. *What happens to the energy in their issues then?*

The possibilities narrow quickly.

The energy in their issues may implode—it may turn within, causing further internal stress and probably becoming, in time, the energy that drives stress disorders such as depression, chronic fatigue, anxiety disorder, etc.

Other than implosion, there is only one other possibility left—

Psychic outletting.

Psychic outletting is the default option. Psychic outletting occurs when the individual has failed to enlist any other way to move the energy within their issues.

As a default phenomenon, psychic outletting is—

✧ Largely unconscious,

✧ Highly irresponsible, and

✧ Invariably messy.

Default phenomena tend to occur automatically. When default conditions exist, the default response occurs, automatically. In the case of psychic outletting this is very unfortunate—a person can outlet their unresolved issue in the form of damaging psychic energy and not even know that they are doing it. Messes ensue. For example, the energy in a person's anger may outlet as psychic barbs that travel in psychic space to the person towards whom the anger was being felt. Or these barbs may travel in psychic space to—who knows for sure?—since psychic outletting is patently sloppy, irresponsible and unconscious, the energy may wind up disturbing the space of other people in highly unpredictable ways. Ironically and very sadly, the person who withholds presence, trust and respect usually has an agenda of *control,* yet by the time the energy in their issues reaches the stage of psychic outletting it can be dangerously out of control.

Events like this are common. Each has a theme or a pattern. Sometimes people psychically cord other people in an effort to control them. Parents often psychically program their children with the same fears and biases that the parents have come to live by. Women who want to look sexually appealing often broadcast psychic energies of allurement to men, and men, in turn, are often sending similar psychic messaging to women. This tends to create an energy climate in which authentic bonding can feel very tenuous and difficult. When two individuals do get together and form a relationship, they may encounter times when misunderstanding and hurt feelings backlog and wind up outletting as psychic energies of resistance, misgiving, blame and antagonism. At this stage, all the couple knows for sure is that the relationship feels like it's not working—but the truth is that the relationship barely stands a chance of working while the two of them are trying to function in a cloud of this type of energy. We could give many other examples of psychic energy patterns.

What Is Psychic Energy?

What *is* all this "psychic energy"? It is simply the energy that originates in people's issues but finally—because the issues are not reckoned with in healthy ways—seeks expression in ulterior ways. The energy degrades. It becomes the stuff of real problems.

Issues, as we have said, are not problems; issues invite our personal growth and healing. Real problems—psychic energy entanglements—tend to degenerate into something very different, into conditions that practically defy healing. This is simply because, typically, the person trying to deal with psychic energy entanglements cannot see them or sense them well enough to get a handle on what's really going on, much less get a handle on how to resolve what's going on. As a result, psychic energy entanglements may persist for a very long time, and lead to multiple layers of wounding, compensations, and complications that, on their own respective levels, may not even have anything to do with the issues that were involved in the original psychic misbehavior.

This is when it is wise to consult a gifted intuitive energy healer who can sort through the landscape of psychic energy entanglements and bring healing at the level where it is most needed, at the level of the original psychic misbehavior.

I will share a memorable example from my own healing work. A fellow from Montana phoned me one day and asked me to help his wife who was suffering from severe neck pain. We'll call her Carol. The doctors had found no cause for Carol's pain and had reached the point of proposing a radical surgery that would fuse two cervical vertebrae together and leave Carol with seriously impaired mobility for the rest of her life—all this in the hopes of lessening her mysterious pain. We scheduled a time for her to call. At the time of the appointment she was in such pain that all she could do was lie in bed, so her husband dialed the number and handed the phone to her. As I tuned in to her case I was drawn to her early teenage years, about age thirteen. I sensed a major trauma occurring around that time but she assured me there had been no major falls or injuries back then. As I tuned in more, I started to sense sexual pain and perhaps even sexual abuse energies. I asked her if she had been sexually hurt or abused when she was thirteen. She started sobbing. Yes, some one had raped her. Apparently her husband didn't even know about this. But it was time to talk about it—in fact the time to talk about it was way past due. As she shared about it, I was shown that the rapist had hurled a psychic threat at her, threatening her to keep silent about the rape. The energy of this threat had lodged in her neck. The neck, as a unique part of our body/mind system, can be all about options and choices—when we turn our head from side to side we command a wide range of options, new directions, etc.—and since the rapist's threat was meant to shut down her sense of options, the threat, as an energy projection, had lodged in her neck.

This energy was *toxic*—so toxic that, over the years, it had literally disabled the normal functioning of Carol's neck.

Awareness promotes healing. As our awareness became clear, finally, on what Carol's challenge was really about, healing light started to mobilize. The rapist's psychic energy, deeply embedded as it was, yielded to the light and was cleared from Carol's neck. Her pain started to lift as well. When the healing session was complete I asked her to keep me informed. A week or two later she called to say that the pain was largely gone and the doctors' new diagnosis had just come in—no need for surgery!

The Road to Healing

But the real healing had only just begun.

The real healing in Carol's case was that now she was on the road to re-empowering herself.

Now she was free to start drawing back into focus
the essential inner work of owning her true power
as a divinely endowed soul.

Now she could start becoming the person who owns her power so well that she simply wouldn't *need* to attract challenges to it anymore, since these challenges were showing up merely to make sure she was doing the essential inner work of *owning her power*.

This deeper level of healing was implicit within her challenged condition and awaited her attention. I heard from Carol only occasionally after her breakthrough session, but learned that her journey of re-empowerment was taking her to, among other new choices, the choice to separate from her husband. I know that, painful as this choice must have been for her, it was helping her find the space to own her power and her unique goodness and beauty. I know that Carol was on the road to *becoming the person* who could give her best and receive the best in any subsequent relationship, whether it be a renewed relationship with her husband or any other relationship she may choose to explore.

We all have to walk the road to healing. We all have essential inner work to do, the work of owning our full potential as divinely endowed souls. When we own our full potential well enough we *become the person* who doesn't need the old issues and problems anymore. Even psychic misbehavior and the extreme complications that may arise from psychic misbehavior shall yield, resolve, and heal as we learn to incarnate our true divine power.

And the particular steps that we need to take along the road to healing are always implicit in our particular challenges. This point is so very important to understand. It means that we can learn a lot by *working with* our challenges, that our challenges are meant to *take us somewhere.*

Challenge Evolves into Healing

In chapters 9 and 10 we saw how *blessing* is a universal spiritual activity that flows from the pure divine love of the infinite Source into all moments equally, including moments of challenge. In chapter 11 we saw how everything in the manifest worlds of form, *everything,* is upheld in form by the passion of the Divine Mother and draws to it the support of Spirit to evolve to its highest expression. And "everything" certainly includes challenge in all its forms, from simple issues to the most painful, entangled problems. *All* challenge draws blessing and support to evolve to its highest expression.

How is it that challenge goes hand in hand with blessing? How is it that challenge *evolves?* And what is the "highest expression" of a challenge?

Challenge evolves into healing.
The highest expression of any challenge
is the ultimate healing or resolution
that is, in fact, always implicit in the energies
within the challenge.

Challenge takes us on the road to healing. But if we withhold or try to just "get rid" of a challenge, we may not achieve authentic healing. The challenge won't have a chance to evolve to the stage of authentic healing. We may succeed in "getting rid" of the outer details of the challenge or the current form of the challenge, but then the energies and themes within the challenge will seek re-expression in a new form that will be likely to appear later on. Most of us probably feel all too familiar with how this works. Even our subtlest thoughts and feelings that cast a challenging situation as something we'd rather push away or get rid of, can sign us up for another round of *different circumstances, same problem.*

However—

As we learn to stay present to the energies
and themes within a challenge,
that's when the challenge can evolve to its highest expression.
That's when the challenge can evolve into healing.

Allowing Healing

Life is all there is. We can allow life or we can resist life. When we choose to withhold or judge, however subtly, we resist life. When we choose to stay present, we allow life.

When we allow life we allow healing.

On Course

The dynamics of conscious presence, awareness, and healing are not meant to run, by the way, on blind trust. The more we refine our ability to stay conscious and present in times of challenge, the more we may start to glimpse the workings of the living Spirit "behind the scenes," as it were, working to evolve our challenged state, painful as it may be feeling to us, into authentic stages of healing. It is very reassuring to glimpse this. I personally have taken great inspiration from little threshold moments when I sense the Sacred Feminine at work, right there in my pain and confusion, guiding it, nurturing it, keeping her promise that "this too" can evolve. The Mother's passion is breathtaking and unforgettable. She *means it* when She promises that all of life, even challenge, shall evolve to its highest expression. She means it when She assures us that *life is all about evolution* and that the time of true healing, when it blossoms, can feel like a rich and welcome flowering of our life-force, a life-force that has been evolving on course, we finally see, by enduring through arduous stages of compression and internal growth before opening at last into beautiful petals of new understanding and compassion, new aliveness and joy.

If we are present we are on course. If we are consciously present, impeccably and unconditionally present, we come to see at last that in God's universe of unlimited sacred aliveness—

- ✧ There is absolutely nothing to worry about; and
- ✧ There is really nothing for us to do but get on with it, get on with evolving our lives.

This is soul freedom.

Chapter 13

Evolution and the Paradigm Shift

Every time healing occurs in our individual lives the human family as a whole moves closer to a major evolutionary leap. Every time healing occurs in our individual lives the human family as a whole moves closer to transforming the whole paradigm or mass consensus by which incarnate life is understood and lived on our planet.

The Old Paradigm—

A Paradigm of Separation and Control

The prevailing paradigm has been predicated on separation. Each individual is seen as separate and on their own. Presence itself is seen as a state of being separate and on one's own—when in truth this condition is anything but authentic presence. It is chronic with-holding. As we said in the last chapter, this condition leaves the individual disconnected from the sacred wholeness of life and leaves the rest of us *missing* him or her. We all came to earth on a soul mission to explore the creative, synergistic, transformational power of divine love, and we need each other to *be here*, soulfully present, coming from love, getting on with why we're here.

The paradigm of separation has persisted through centuries of human life on the planet simply because it offers the human psyche a functional foundation for practicing *control*. Why does the instinct to control run so deep in the human psyche? Because of threat. Because control seems to help us mitigate anxiety in the face of perceived threat—and the very survival of human life on the planet, especially in earlier stages of evolution, has relied on finding ways to deal with threats, very real threats. But there is a bugaboo here, a downside with consequences that have severely challenged the overall evolution of human consciousness. This downside lies in the simple fact that—

Over time, the paradigm of separation can produce a state
in which everything is perceived as threatening,
since everything is seen as separate from oneself.

Hence the paradigm-bound psyche tends to approach life as an arena of threats and potential threats to be managed by ever-more sophisticated methods of control. *Withholding*, as we are understanding it here, *is such a method of control.* To whatever degree the paradigm-bound psyche may feel threatened—by people who have a different way of life or a different way of looking at life, for example, or by the unpredictable forces of nature and the natural environment, or by a pace of change that is seen as too liberal, or by people displaying shades of emotion and feeling it doesn't really understand— this old, entrenched psyche may seek comfort by trying to control such things.

Yet the greatest threats lie within ourselves. We often, for example, don't really understand our *own* emotions and feelings. The old paradigm-bound psyche is easily threatened by these emotions and feelings too.

The old paradigm-bound psyche is threatened by
the tension within our own unresolved issues,
by the fear and uncertainty, by the layers of
unworthiness, neediness, anger, hurt, and judgment
that press for attention within our unresolved issues.

These layered emotions have persisted in form all along, awaiting our greater awareness and presence so that they can follow the evolutionary imperative to evolve into healing. And heal they must. But the old, controlling psyche is threatened by this too. It feels threatened by the very summons that sounds within our issues, the summons to stop withholding and be present, to drop our defenses and show up, to get back into the sacred loop of giving, to bring all of ourselves to the moment, not just the parts that feel the pain and feel threatened by the pain but the parts that know how to surrender and seek re-connection with something greater than our threatened selves, that know—

How to be tender, how to trust,
how to bless unconditionally,
how to stay true to love.

The threatened psyche may prefer to not have to deal with tenderness and trust, with connectedness and love. The threatened psyche may seek to suppress these redeeming elements and even to disconnect itself or divorce itself from them.

Can it succeed in creating such a fundamental fragmentation, such a negation of the wholeness of human nature? Ultimately, it cannot. But as long as its methods of separation and suppression and control are supported by the very paradigm that has been allowed to prevail on this planet for centuries, the threatened psyche is likely to keep on trying.

Rape is an extreme expression of separation, suppression, and control.

We need to see the rapist as what he is. The rapist is simply the disturbed element in the human psyche that has been trying to function in an old paradigm that cannot work, a paradigm of separation wounds, chronic withholding, and constant threat. The rapist is the profoundly disturbed element that has come to see, finally, that in order for its methods of separation, suppression, and control to survive it needs to attack the feminine, the feminine principle of life—the tenderness and togetherness and wholeness and love.

Rape—the act of attacking tenderness and togetherness and wholeness and love—has become an implicit characteristic of old paradigm consciousness. By its strategies of suppressing and withholding, it violates the natural wholeness of life. It attacks the Sacred Feminine principle itself when it seeks, through chronic withholding and separation behaviors, to breach the natural synergy of life and to dishonor the promise that all of life, even our separation wounds, invites our loving awareness and presence so that all can evolve to total healing.

As such, rape may express equally in both men and in women.

Most of all, this attack on the Sacred Feminine expresses on the level of the collective consciousness, which is precisely where old paradigm patterns are most deeply and chronically ingrained.

The New Paradigm—
A Paradigm of Wholeness
and Authentic Presence

Ultimately rape, as we are understanding it here, is a cry for help. Ultimately this state of awareness *knows* that it needs help desperately. It knows that its desperate survival strategies must fail, that true survival can never occur in a state of extreme fragmentation.

It knows that survival can only occur in a state of wholeness.

It knows it needs a new paradigm. It needs a paradigm in which it no longer attacks the feminine but *reconciles* with the feminine principle and *re-connects with tenderness and togetherness and love.* It needs a paradigm in which it can *rediscover wholeness.*

Human life on the planet is in the midst of precisely this paradigm shift.

The stakes have grown just about as high as they can go. That is why we are seeing signs on the planet, in many disturbing ways, that the old paradigm is being carried to its implicit limits—near destruction of the wholeness of human nature and of human life on the planet as we know it—just so that this paradigm itself can finally attract healing and yield to a new paradigm of love and wholeness.

In the new paradigm—

✧ Separation wounds (judgment, anger, sadness, neediness, unworthiness and fear) invite awareness and presence and evolve to healing.

✧ Resisting life yields to allowing life. Control yields to trust and unconditional aliveness.

✧ Suppression of the feminine yields to the ascendancy of the Sacred Feminine.

- ✧ Dishonor and abuse yield to kindness, generosity, compassion and respect.
- ✧ Separation yields to interconnectedness and wholeness.
- ✧ Most of all, *withholding yields to authentic presence.*

Authentic Presence

In the new paradigm,[7] presence is no longer about separation, control, and withholding. In the new paradigm—

Presence is about coming unconditionally alive
in the sacred wholeness of life,
in the interconnectedness of all things,
and participating in the evolution of life
with the full breadth and depth of who we really are
as divinely commissioned souls,
as incarnations of the living Spirit.

---

7 We will have more to say about the paradigm shift in Chapter 17.

Chapter 14

Incarnating the Living Spirit

Spiritual awakening is rich with complementarity and synergy. As we awaken, we discover how all the parts of life can harmonize and fit together in a divinely inspired matrix of sacred aliveness. We see that life is not divided up into good things and bad things, things to bless and things to judge, but that life subsists, rather, in a natural state of wholeness where all the parts synergistically enrich each other and enrich the whole.

So far, we have explored a number of ways in which spiritual awakening reveals the synergistic nature of things, including—

⋄ Reality is quantum in nature: consciousness imprints the material world, and the material world, in turn, reflects what is going on in our consciousness.

⋄ Love only grows. The more of it we give, the more of it we have. The more love we give to each other, the more love we receive from our common Source. The surest way to receive is to give.

⋄ Life subsists in a sacred loop of giving: as we give to life, life gives back to us. Presence supports life and life supports presence: as we give the gift of authentic presence and respect, life gives back the gift of support and nurturing.

✧ The masculine aspect of Spirit expresses the divine potentials of life and the feminine aspect of Spirit embodies them and nurtures life to its highest evolution.

✧ Challenge in all of its forms participates in evolution and serves evolution. Challenge is never "negative" or counter-evolutionary.

"Rainbow Beings"

There is one more very important synergistic principle to explore here—

✧ The more we ground our individual lives and our individual presence here in the incarnate plane or third-dimensional, earth plane, the more Spirit pours its universal sacred aliveness into us from the higher-dimensional or spiritual planes. In other words, the more we show up, the more Spirit shows up—in us.

As Spirit shows up in us, our whole sense of what it means to be present spirals into new and heightened stages of awakening. We learn to host the living Spirit, to incarnate, consciously, this ineffable Higher Presence that, even as it indwells us in time and space, abides eternally in higher realms.

We become meeting points of heaven and earth, "rainbow" beings, bridges between Spirit and matter. In Native American lore, one of the original words for "human" means, literally, *rainbow.*

Expanding Our Energy State

Energetically, we learn to host the living Spirit by *expanding our energy state* so that we can receive more spiritual energy blessings and integrate more of the heightened vibration of Spirit.

Our energy state may expand in many different ways. Our energy state may expand, for example, when—

- ✧ We let go of the conditional approach to happiness (see Chapter 4).
- ✧ We tune in to the sacred aliveness within the cells of our bodies and feel our cells stirring and swelling to affirm and "cell-ebrate" the pure sanctity of the life-force within us (Chapter 6).
- ✧ We refresh or re-set our awareness to participate in the living truth of Higher Mind (Chapter 7).
- ✧ We transcend the conditional approach to love and quicken our awareness to the vibration of the divine soul consciousness that loves unconditionally (Chapter 8).
- ✧ We transcend judgment, stay present to challenge, and stay true to love and wholeness (Chapters 9 and 10).
- ✧ We tune to the passion of the Sacred Feminine, transcend the drama of separation and trouble, and quicken to the Mother's healing truth that all of life is one (Chapter 11).
- ✧ We re-awaken to the complete and total soul freedom that Spirit endows into each new moment by practicing grounded, present-time presence (Chapter 12).

It is grounded presence, in turn, that prepares us for the most direct and powerful way in which to expand our energy state, when—

✧ We refresh our direct connection to the infinite Spirit by awakening our crown chakra.

Quickening the Crown Chakra

As we learn to be powerfully present and to attract new energy blessings from Spirit, our crown chakra naturally responds, opens, *quickens* to receive the influx of new energy. Much as the base chakra is about our relationship with the earth plane and how to be comfortably functional in the earth plane, the crown chakra is about our relationship with the spiritual planes and how to be comfortably functional in the spiritual planes. The base chakra and the crown chakra are meant to work together. When the base and the crown are awakened, invigorated, and working well together, our experience of *what it means to be present* rises to a higher turn on the spiral of conscious evolution.

Tune your awareness, as before, to the base chakra at the base of your spine, and let it open once again into a fuller, more conscious state of communion with the earth and with all the energies of the earth. Let this grow. Let yourself feel, as before, that you are really showing up, centered, composed, grounded, *present.*

Now let your awareness move comfortably to the top of your head. Tune your awareness to the energy center at the top of your head, to the crown chakra. Feel how responsive *this* chakra is. Feel how, the more centered and present you become, the more your crown chakra wants to expand and open and come alive.

Let your crown chakra respond now, let it open and expand and come more alive. Let this be easy and natural. Your crown knows what to do. You are opening to new energies, energies of support and blessing from the spiritual planes. Your whole energy state can be refreshed or "re-set" to spiritual presence and spiritual principle. Your awareness can expand naturally to participate in the activity of the living Spirit. See if you can feel this now. The activity of the living Spirit is both timeless and now. It resonates with wisdom and beauty and sacredness. Open into this. Participate. Life is naturally whole, naturally sacred. We are deeply connected to the sacredness. We are never alone. We are sponsored and supported in our individual presence as expressions of the universal sacred aliveness. Our individual lives participate in the universal sacred aliveness. Spirit is simply this "Higher Presence" of infinite sacred aliveness. Spirit is right here, right now. Spirit is as present here and now—in you—as anywhere or anytime. Your personal awareness *hosts* the Infinite. Your personal presence *incarnates* the Infinite.

This experience can be a powerful event, a time of spiritual invigoration and vibrational lifting. When the crown chakra quickens, our energy state can expand dramatically with the currents of new aliveness coming in. We feel flushed with greater presence, refreshed and even pleasured in how good this feels. Refined frequencies of light and love are awakening refined new states of awareness in us and this awareness is spreading and expanding like leaven through our brain/mind. Our whole being, as we let the crown chakra really quicken, goes into a kind of *spiritual energy arousal.*

We are coming alive in the Spirit.

When the crown chakra quickens, *all* of the chakras start to respond and to come more fully "online" to participate in the energy blessings and energy upgrades. If we have been doing a good job of developing our grounded presence, in the body, in present time, in our love and gratitude, now the Higher Presence can truly indwell us and awaken its gifts in us. If we have been using our grounding to let go of the weighted and clunky patterns in us that were trying to run on something other than spiritual principle, now the Higher Presence can restore our consciousness to spiritual principle. Now we can upgrade. We can let our separation wounds yield to love and wholeness. We can let our conditional beliefs and agendas for happiness yield to unconditional frequencies of pure happiness. The experience of pure, unconditional happiness becomes astonishingly simple when we come alive in the Spirit. Our uncertainty, doubt, and confusion can yield to new currents of living wisdom and the blessings that living wisdom bestows: guidance, discernment, vision, elevated purpose, and conviction. Our control issues can yield to the authentic creative power of the indwelling Spirit. Our neediness can yield to certainty and havingness, the certainty of knowing that we already have unlimited good endowed into our true inner nature. Our anxiety can yield to peace, the authentic peace of the Infinite. Our fear can yield to trust. *All* of our patterns of resistance can yield to pure frequencies of sacred aliveness.

And we realize, once again, that we are free. We are free to be alive unconditionally, to love unconditionally, to be happy unconditionally, to have our good unconditionally, to participate unconditionally in all the gifts of the Higher Presence.

Tune in once again. You are alive and free, grounded and present, your lower chakras are open, your crown chakra is open as well, you are an open system, open above, open below, commingling the energies of heaven and earth.

You are extraordinarily *present*.

Expanding Our Identity

But who are you? *Who* is present?

Good question! This is the real question and the central issue of our existence—who are we, really?

Be with the question.

If the question moves you into thoughts that who you are is somehow *less* than this extraordinary presence, *less* than this extraordinary, embodied, individuated, ground-ed presence of the pure unconditional aliveness and au-thentic peace and wisdom and power and joy and light and love and exquisite wholeness of the Infinite—then the expanded energy state that you have been vibrat-ing in contracts. The heightened arousal state stalls and contracts.

You may feel a sensation of *strain*.

See if you can let go of the sense of a lesser, or finite, or troubled identity.

See if you can surrender any such identity, familiar as it may be, back into a more expanded state of pres-ence. See if you can shift back into the conscious state of hosting the Infinite, of incarnating the Higher Presence. How to accomplish this? Focus at the crown chakra. The crown knows how to ply our relationship with the Higher Presence. Let the crown open and expand. Welcome once again the heightened energy state that opening the crown takes you into.

Balance this with your grounding. Stay grounded, even as you move once again into the state of expanded aliveness and presence.

Notice that when you expand your energy state in this way, your more accustomed sense of yourself tends to slip out of focus. Your more limited sense of yourself, with its accustomed abc's—agendas, beliefs, conditions— for a more accustomed style of aliveness and presence, tends to slip from your awareness.

Can you be okay with this?

Can you trust? Can you be unafraid of having the familiar agendas, beliefs and conditions of the accustomed, limited self slip out of focus?

Can you trust that expanded aliveness and presence will not confound who you really are?

Can you let the whole question about who you really are be an open question?

And can you, meanwhile, keep opening to Spirit *for the sake of Spirit?*

Developing Trust

Tune to your crown. See your crown as a *trust muscle*. Imagine your crown is a muscle or sphincter that can expand and contract, open and close.

✧ When your crown opens, you feel the joy of hosting and incarnating the living Spirit.

✧ When your crown closes, you feel the strain of separation from Spirit.

Feel the difference. Try it both ways. Really feel the difference.

Two Masters

Clearly, this chakra cannot be both open and closed at the same time. When the crown is open it cannot be closed, and when it is closed it cannot be open. One state excludes the other. And so we have a choice. The axiom that "You cannot serve two masters" is very meaningful here. In the life of the crown chakra, in the energetics of our relationship with the higher planes, the two masters are—

✧ *Trust,* versus

✧ Fear.

Just as a chakra cannot be both open and closed at the same time, our consciousness cannot vibrate in both trust and fear at the same time. One excludes the other. When we are in trust we cannot be in fear. When we are in fear we cannot be in trust. Trust allows life. Trust opens us into the state of being radically and unconditionally alive and joyous. Fear resists life. Fear puts conditions on our aliveness and joy. We cannot both allow life and resist life at the same time. Trust affirms there is something bigger than ourselves, trust affirms the sacred wholeness of which we are a part. Fear asserts separation and clings desperately to the smaller, separate self. Trust is, by its nature, a radical spiritual practice; trust is radical and unconditional. Fear is, by its nature, the antithesis of turning to Spirit; fear is getting lost in conditions.

When we trust, we feel the joy of hosting and incarnating the infinite living Spirit. When we fear, we feel the strain of separation from the living Spirit.

Tune to your crown. Feel your choices. How will you choose to be present?

If this feels right for you now, let your crown quicken, let it expand more and more, like a trust muscle that is getting truly fit. Feel your trust. Feel your trust opening you into the greater reality, into the universal sacred aliveness. Expand into this. Open into the heightened reality in which *who you are*, in the synergies of learning to be present in this multi-dimensional universe of living energies, *has everything to do with what the universe itself is.* Open into this. Be a part of the whole. Be a conscious participant in this Higher Presence of universal sacred aliveness.

You cannot serve two masters. Trust expands you into the universal sacred aliveness. Fear separates you from it. If your trust feels truly right to you now, *choose* it.

*Choose a style of presence
in which your identity expands
to participate in the Higher Presence,
in the universal sacred aliveness,
as a part of the whole, as a conscious incarnation
of the infinite, living Spirit.*

Chapter 15

Taking the Leap—
Transcending
the Conditional Self

We often mark our progress along the path of spiritual awakening by how well and how often, how regularly and reliably we are experiencing ourselves as free and joyous participants in the unconditional sacred aliveness of the living Spirit. As our experience of being alive and present quickens to incarnate, consciously, more and more of the Higher Presence, we learn that we must—

Entrust to the Higher Presence
the whole question of exactly who we are.

Our trust is well placed. And the more trust we develop, the better. We are going to need it.

Meanwhile, we get to keep discovering how freeing it feels to keep opening to Spirit for the sake of Spirit rather than for the sake of what some separate "self" of ours could get from the experience.

Spiritual Discernment

Trust placed in the Higher Presence is not undiscerning, blind, or wishful, but quite the opposite. Trust placed in Spirit is eminently discerning. On our path of spiritual awakening we are meant to learn that trust and discernment go hand in hand. The more we place our trust in Spirit, the more we awaken into spiritual discernment.

We are going to need it.

Taking the Leap

There is a much-loved story from the lore surrounding the Indian saint Babaji, a highly realized master to whom many miraculous events are ascribed. It seems there was a fellow in the area where Babaji was spending time who made up his mind that he simply must become one of Babaji's disciples. So one day he approached the master and implored, "Babaji, Babaji, make me your disciple!"

"Fine, just jump off this cliff," said Babaji, indicating a nearby precipice.

The aspirant looked over the edge of the cliff and saw that it was a long, steep drop to jagged rocks. "But master," he said, "if I jump I will surely die!"

Babaji was impassive.

The man slumped away in frustration.

After a few days the aspirant got his courage up and approached the master again. "Babaji, Babaji, please make me your disciple!"

Babaji could see that the man was patently attached to his desire. "Fine, just jump off this cliff."

"But if I jump off the cliff I will surely die!"

Babaji was impassive.

This went on for several rounds. Each time the aspirant approached the master he was disheartened to be told to jump off the cliff, so he slumped away in abject frustration. Finally one day the aspirant had a change of heart. "Wait a minute," he thought, "if the master says jump, why don't I jump? I want to show my devotion to him don't I? That's what it's about isn't it?"

He approached Babaji. When Babaji said jump, he jumped. His body hit the rocks below and instantly perished. Babaji made his way down to where the battered body lay, brought it back to life, and made the man his disciple.

They could have done this on the first day! But the aspirant needed a little more time to work through his issues, develop his trust, and open to the master's message.

The Master Within

In this story and all such stories about great teachers, the master in the story represents what we might call the master within us. And the master within, the voice of pure divine wisdom that lives at the core of all of us, can guide our lives with the same impeccable spiritual wisdom as any realized teacher in the world. Basically, the master's message to us is—

> *Get in touch with the part of you that is mortal*
> *and let go of it.*
> *It is not the real you.*

What is it in the aspirant's nature that is mortal and must be let go of?

Obviously, the aspirant's physical body fits this description. And the Babaji/aspirant story, like all death and rebirth legends and myths, conveys the transcendence of the physical body—but ultimately goes to a much deeper level.

So on a deeper level, what is it in the aspirant that is mortal and must be let go of?

Wherever There Is Mind...

Is it the conditioned mind, we may ask, that had so befuddled the aspirant that he needed to let go of it? As long as the aspirant was caught up in conditioned thinking, he was struggling. "I must become Babaji's disciple. I will not be happy until I am Babaji's disciple. If I jump off the cliff I will die. If I die I cannot become Babaji's disciple. How will I ever be happy then?" This is a classic case of conditioned mind entrapment.

Yet from the start, all the aspirant needed to do was to shift from his contracted or conditioned state of mind to a higher, more expanded state of mind—then he was free to see that the path to fulfillment lay graciously before him.

So is the problem the conditioned mind?

...There Is the One Mind

Recall the old Buddhist expression quoted in Chapter 7, "Wherever there is mind, there is the One Mind." The conditioned mind is included in this. *Wherever* there is mind, there is the One Mind, whether it be mind vibrating in the frequency range that we understand as "conditioned," or mind vibrating in the frequency range that we understand as "Higher."

Mind is created by Spirit. Mind is the arena in which the infinite creative potentials of Spirit play and express.

And Mind is not mortal.

Mind Expands, Mind Contracts

The main difference between conditioned mind and Higher Mind is a relative matter of expanded energy versus contracted energy.

✧ When mind is in a more expanded energy state, it participates purely in universal truth. This is "Higher Mind."

When we are in this state we *know* that we are part of the universal reality or the "One Mind."

✧ When mind is in a more contracted energy state, it will tend to participate less purely in the play of universal truth. It may select, it may edit, it may even strain to get the flux of creative potentials to match its concerns. Under the strain, what often ensues is distortion. This is the realm of conditioned mind.

In this state we tend to forget that we are a part of the whole.

Over time, our minds will tend to vibrate in *all* possible frequency ranges, much like an ocean will tend to swell, over time, in all possible wave formations. As we said in an earlier chapter, life itself is simply the play and interplay of infinite creative potentials.

Sometimes the mind naturally expresses in the more contracted ranges. Contraction occurs naturally whenever the mind focuses on the necessary business of taking care of our human needs. When we become hungry, for example, the mind focuses on supplying nutrition to the body and thoughts like "I'll feel better when I get something to eat," or "I do my best work when I've had a good lunch," or "If I don't follow the doctor's recommendations for regular meals and snacks I may develop blood sugar problems like he talked about" may naturally occur. Such thoughts occur in the frequency range of conditioned mind, as they postulate that "I'll be okay as certain conditions are met." The conditioned mind is continually checking on our okayness. That's its job. We might say it this way—

The conditioned mind plays a natural role
of navigating our progress through the experience
of being human.

Feeling Okay Is Condition-Sensitive

Let's look at an example that is a little more complicated than simply getting hungry. Let's look at an example from the emotional side of being human. Suppose you are involved in a meaningful conversation with some one. Both you and he are warming to the experience of communicating, sharing your feelings, learning from each other. Then something happens that doesn't feel quite okay to you. While you are speaking, an innocent little distraction occurs—perhaps the cat meows or the breeze picks up or perhaps you just sense that a momentary lapse of attention passes like a cloud over the other person's awareness—and you start to wonder whether he has quite heard what you were sharing. We like to be heard. We like to be received. You start to wonder whether he is nodding his head just to be nice. Your mind contracts a bit. "Am I quite okay with what just happened? Should I ask him if he understands—or would that be impolite? Should I repeat myself, or would that be awkward? Should I just forget about it? But then he may not really appreciate what I've been sharing. Should I settle for feeling sort of okay but sort of uncertain?" We are probably all familiar with moments like this.

The thoughts that flicker in our minds at moments like this are occurring in the frequency range of the conditioned mind. They postulate that our emotional okayness is *condition-sensitive.*

Condition-sensitive moments like this occur all the time. They occur innocently, and they can be managed innocently. In relatively simple cases we adapt without getting hung up. We manage the moment. That's the point—

> *Our minds naturally expand and contract*
> *to manage our okayness*
> *through fluctuating life circumstances.*

In the example given above, chances are that we will innocently relax out of our little contractive moment and get on with enjoying rapport with our friend as best the circumstances will allow. Circumstances are always changing anyhow. The point is that our minds keep adapting, and that our minds can do this innocently, naturally, and, most important of all, appropriately.

Contraction is certainly appropriate at times. Under challenging circumstances our awareness may contract *a lot.* But the dance doesn't need to get complicated unless this contraction causes us to lose our more expanded state of mind. Managing our human needs is one thing, but—

As spiritual beings we need to be able
to sustain our true sense of ourselves
in the more expanded frequency ranges of awareness.

It's in the more expanded frequency ranges of awareness that we access living wisdom and unconditional happiness. This is where we access compassionate presence and authentic healing. This is where we feel our indwelling sacred aliveness and stay centered in our natural state of soul freedom.

So the key to human awareness is balance, learning to balance contracted awareness with expanded awareness.

Unfortunately, when the mind moves into its more contracted or conditioned range we often tend to *over-identify* with the experience we're in, and then we slip out of balance. We may get swept up in how the experience is triggering certain feelings in us. These feelings may stir up a storm of worrisome thoughts and angles and contingencies, blowing us off center. We may get caught up in certain angles, or even fascinated by them. We may invest. We may get fascinated by our mind's sheer ability to cascade more and more contingencies. We may get swept up in *managing* all the contingencies and conditions. We may get tense and self-involved about it all. We may try to make the whole experience we're having more important than, in the big picture, it really is. In effect, we are getting carried away with *staking our okayness* on the subjective experience we're having.

Worse, we may confuse our okayness with our happiness.

We may lose sight of the fact that true well being, true happiness, lies beyond conditions, no matter how well the conditions may or may not be managed.

All this does not go unnoticed by the Master within.

Discernment Time

The Master within, the voice of living wisdom, will seek ways to remind us, at times like this, that we simply must start discerning what is going on. We must discern what it is in us that holds us in contraction and confounds our true happiness.

We must discern what it is in us that is mortal and errant, what it is that lives in us or that seeks to have a life in us, however provisional, however conditional, however mortal—and then we must see that this form of conditional aliveness has simply got to be transcended.

At times like this the conditioned mind may *seem* like the mortal, errant part of us.

But it is not.

Identification Instinct

If there is anything errant behind all the drama, it lies in what we might call the identification instinct.

Recall what we said in the previous chapter about identity. When our awareness is functioning freely in more expanded states, our sense of identity expands too. In the previous chapter we explored this especially with regard to quickening the crown chakra and coming alive in Spirit. At these times we naturally sense that who we are is intimately and profoundly involved with hosting the Higher Presence. We sense our identity as an individual incarnation of the living Spirit.

If we can be comfortable with this,
if we can trust that we are a part of the whole and that,

ultimately, who we are has everything to do with
the higher reality of what the universe itself is,
then our identification instinct is simply relaxed, quiescent.

We feel no particular desire, at moments like this, to define a more personal sense of self or to separate a personal self out from the wholeness that we are experiencing. We are carried in the wholeness. We are happy to be a part of the whole and a participant in the whole.

But when our awareness is straining in more contracted energy states, our sense of identity may contract too. The more unsettled and uncertain we feel about what is going on, the more unsettled and uncertain we may feel about who we are. This is when the identification instinct comes into play. Basically, we discover that we can bring a bit more definition or definite-ness into our sense of who we are by simply *identifying into what is going on.* We discover, that is, that we can *project a sense of identity, or self, into our responses in the world.* We can create an "I" in the midst of what is going on. As we adapt and respond to the world in our unique ways, we assert, "This is *me."* We assert the "I" in many diverse ways, from "I get along okay as long as I keep an eye on my blood sugar levels" (condition), to "I have something worthwhile to say and I want to be heard" (agenda), to "I just know I'll be happy if only Babaji would make me his disciple" (belief)...to...the ways in which we assert an "I" become myriad. Our assertions of an "I" tend to grow out of conditioned mind perspectives, and to identify into the abc's—agendas, beliefs, and conditions—of the conditioned mind.

Out of all this, we start to develop a functional sense of identity in the world. We usually like how this feels. We feel that we are starting to enjoy a certain baseline okayness founded on having this well-defined "I." And so we reinforce the instinct to—

Identify into our responses to the world
so that we can keep feeling a functional sense of
identity in the world.

Identification Phenomenon

All this may seem innocent enough on its own level. But the bugaboo about identification is that it tends to feed itself. The more we interpret as positive this growing feeling of having a solid sense of self in the world, the more the feeling grows. The "I" attracts attention to itself and grows stronger.

Soon enough the "I" wants to take over. It wants to control our inner state of mind.

This "I" seeks ways to override the voice of wisdom, the still small voice within that would say "Wait a minute, the real Self is born of Spirit, not of mere adaptations in the world. The real Self is bigger than any personal identity in the world. The real Self doesn't need to stake its happiness on agendas, beliefs, and conditions. You cannot grasp what the real Self is until you grasp what the higher or spiritual reality of the universe itself is."

The "I" does not want to hear that it is errant. The "I" would rather find ways to confound the voice of wisdom. The "I" may in fact become very shrewd and cunning about keeping the mind stuck in contractive frequency ranges. The "I" may identify into layer upon familiar layer of contractive thoughts and feelings—judgment, anger, sadness, neediness, inadequacy, fear, and, ultimately, separation. The "I" knows that when our awareness is struggling in separation wounds and separation dramas it tends to lose the big picture.

This "I" is commonly known, of course, as the *ego*. It is the conditional self, the limited self that identifies into separation and a conditional approach to life.

As we awaken, we discern that—

The ego is not a true identity.

We see that, rather—

The ego is merely an identification phenomenon.

As we awaken we learn to discern the difference between *true iden-tity* and a mere *identification phenomenon*. We see that ego is merely an apparent form or phenomenon, a provisional identity, *a condi-tional self born of an errant identification instinct*. And so we come to see that—

The ego is a false identity.

All phenomena are temporary—or if you will, mortal. What then is the part of us that the voice of living wisdom has been exhorting us to discern as mortal? What is the part of us that we must learn to let go of at all costs?

Ego.

At All Costs

Why is the voice of living wisdom, the Master within, so uncompro-mising on this point? Because a life ruled by ego is, simply, a life of unfulfillment. Egoic agendas will never produce true happiness. Egoic agendas are patently conditional, while true happiness is un-conditional. In the Babaji myth, if Babaji had made the aspirant his disciple while the man was still attached to his agenda, the poor man *still* would not have been happy. Happiness would always elude him.

We *cannot* find true happiness as long as we are putting conditions, no matter how lofty, on how we want to have our happiness. Conditions always change. This is the first and most fundamental of the four "noble truths" of Buddhism—*dukkha,* the pain of impermanence. Conditions are always changing.

Life itself will press the issue. As we have said throughout this book—

✧ Life is all there is, and the only real choice we have is between allowing life and resisting life.
✧ Life must evolve.
✧ Life beckons us to let go of our resistance, let go of the conditional approach to happiness, and allow ourselves to really come alive *without* conditions—radically alive, unconditionally alive.

We must apply these principles radically. We must free our awareness to discover, to deeply and passionately grasp, that—

✧ Life is real, but ego is not real. Life subsists in sacred wholeness, while ego resists wholeness. Ego invests in separation, but wholeness is what is real.
✧ Life evolves, but ego does not evolve.
✧ Life is guided and evolved by living wisdom, but ego is driven by fear, the fear of separation.

As we grasp what this really means we start to realize that something is going to have to give here. We start to realize that life is going to ask us to face our fear. One way or another, sooner or later, life is going to orchestrate circumstances in order to summon us to take the leap, to die to our false, fear-driven, egoic selves, and to come alive in the only reality that is permanent and enduring—unconditional, undistorted, unwounded, unlimited universal sacred aliveness.

Life Is a Master Teacher

Our lives are shaped and directed by the same evolutionary imperative that directs the universe. Sometimes we allow this evolutionary force more, sometimes we allow it less. All along, life is intent on teaching us to discern the path to happiness, for—

Life is too adept a guide
to let us find happiness in a false identity.

Life says, "Sorry, you don't get to be that person. You may pursue the false identity, you may pursue it and develop it and build it up all you want, but you won't turn out to *be* the false identity and ultimately you won't find real happiness in it." We have all known disappointment, we have all encountered our own, unique times to sorrow in *dukkha,* the pain of impermanence. Life just keeps altering our circumstances to keep prodding us and prompting us to seek out the happiness that lies beyond all circumstances, to find the true happiness that is unconditional.

Our lives become a sort of running discernment drill. We learn to keep logging the messages, "Sorry you don't get to be the person who finds true happiness in *this* conditional identity," and "Sorry you don't get to be the person who finds true happiness in *that* limited identity." The lessons get pretty rigorous. We tend to want to try one conditional identity after another—which only leads to one "Sorry" after another. But if we can stay undaunted, if we can learn to flow with the essential evolutionary rigor that life seeks to hold us to, if we can learn to not take life's lessons too personally, we can awaken into conscious soul freedom.

We can learn to engage the experience of life, itself, as the most advanced discernment drill or "*neti, neti*" practice we could ever have. (In some of the Vedantic teachings of India, seekers are taught to transcend false identities by constantly repeating "neti, neti," which means "I am not this, I am not that.") Each time we get the message, each time we let go of conditional identity and draw nearer to the precipice, we draw nearer to unconditional aliveness and conscious soul freedom.

Ultimately, life itself can subsume all spiritual paths and systems of inquiry, whether Vedantic or Babaji-based or any other. Life itself turns out to be that powerful, simply because life is driven by the evolutionary imperative of the whole universe. And since life itself can subsume all paths, seekers of liberation and true happiness don't have to stake their success on finding the right teacher or the right teaching. *None of us have to stake our evolution on finding a specific, "right" teacher or teaching.* Life itself can evolve us all the way. As we said at the very outset of this book, life is a totally radical matter.

The only issue is, how radically have we given ourselves to the experience of life?

It is compelling to understand that, if we are hedging, if we are nursing a conditional, separate self that withholds from life, life *still* evolves.

> *Life keeps evolving,*
> *but it seeks evolution, if we resist,*
> *through <u>other</u> individuals and <u>other</u> life-forms.*

That's how little stock this radical thing called life places in the conditional, separate, egoic self! In fact—

The evolutionary force of life is ultimately impersonal.

The evolutionary force of life doesn't really care if it gets to express and unfold through any of us, as individuals. But if we can "get out of our own way," if we can let go of our personal stake in conditional agendas, if we can transcend the fear and withholding patterns of our conditional, egoic self, *then* life will evolve us all the way into conscious soul freedom. Life evolves us all the way—when we get *out* of the way.

Life Evolves, Ego Does Not Evolve

When it comes to evolution, the ultimate authority is Divine Mother, the universal Sacred Feminine, Who lives within all evolving things as the very essence of their nurturance and growth. Her perspective is paramount. In the perspective of the Divine Mother—

Nothing at all in the design of the universe
will support the evolution of the ego.

In the perspective of the Mother—

Ego simply does not evolve.

In fact Divine Mother does not even recognize ego. She recognizes everything else. She recognizes all of our evolutionary desires, and lovingly upholds them. She recognizes all of our issues as well, and compassionately upholds them so that they can invite our conscious presence and evolve into healing. But She will not uphold our false identity, She will not uphold our ego. Her position on the matter is fierce, as only the cosmic Mother can be fierce. Everything that exists in this universe must be co-created out of the infinite divine potentials of the Source. Once we co-create something out of the infinite divine potentials of the Source, She will support its evolution. She will freely supply Her precious love and nurturance for it to evolve. But She draws the line at ego; She does not recognize ego or false identity as something that can arise out of Source. Source is infinite Presence, unconditional Higher Presence, and ego is false presence, which is no presence at all. Ego is not real. No matter how familiar it may seem to us at times, the limited, conditional self that we have projected into our responses in the world, is not real and enduring.

Yes, this is radical. Yes, this draws us to the precipice.

And yes, as we take the leap a new life awaits us, the only life that is real and enduring, the only life that matches our true soul identity— life in freedom, life in unconditional, undistorted, unwounded, unlimited universal sacred aliveness and soul freedom.

Chapter 16

Conscious Soul Freedom

Neil was the type of person who loved to make a difference. Whenever Neil spoke you could hear the deep compassion and caring in his voice. He shared with the rest of the group on Mt. Shasta, one summer, how much he wanted to make a difference in his family, in his community back home in Virginia, and especially in the state of the world. He was a natural visionary. He envisioned a time when everyone lives consciously from their Source and shares themselves soulfully, from their essence.

The universe loves to use individuals who want to make a difference.

That summer's gathering at Mt. Shasta was drawing near a close. The next day was to be our last full day together on the mountain. "Is the group up for a longer hike tomorrow?" I asked. "It'll be well worth it if you're all up for it." I had in mind a secluded meadow with extraordinary spiritual energy and a spring that flows through the meadow and then descends, just below the meadow itself, into a cascade of magical waterfalls. We talked about the logistics of the hike, the need to allow more time, etc., and decided—let's go for it!

Neil had a gleam in his eye.

The next day, as we hiked, Neil reminded us of the three crystals he had brought with him from Virginia. "I don't know whether I chose them or they chose me, but they wanted to come to this mountain with me," he said. Crystals of course can hold and amplify our intention and our vision. Neil said he had felt a strong intuition that the crystals belonged on Mt. Shasta, that they would somehow play a role or make a difference, by seeding the subtle energy planes with his vision of a more enlightened east coast, for example.

By today, Neil had already placed two of the three crystals at spots on the mountain where he sensed they were meant to be. He still carried the third crystal in his pocket.

We got to the meadow, explored, dipped in the spring, workshopped, ate lunch. Then we headed downstream. We came to a little spot on the banks of the waterfall where the otherwise steep, rugged terrain leveled off to form just enough space for the dozen or so of us to gather. We spent a little time tuning in to the energies. Then Neil spoke up. "This is the spot," he said, "right out there." He pointed to the middle of the waterfall where the spring water was hurtling over rocks and fallen logs and the hearty blooming plants that thrive in the spray.

"This time I want everybody to be involved," he said. Earlier in the week he had placed his other crystals without directly involving the group.

Now he cupped the third crystal in his hands. Suddenly his voice filled with emotion. "I'm feeling guided to just hold the crystal for a moment and put all of myself into it. Then each of us take a turn."

The crystal passed hands with an almost solemn feeling of ritual. Each one of us felt a sudden resonance and depth of emotion as we took our turn instilling our energy into the crystal. In some unspoken way, it seemed to really *matter* that we get our essence into that crystal.

Then it was time to help Neil get out to the center of the waterfall. We formed a human bridge. Most of the group anchored the bridge on the banks. Neil stepped out to the first rock or stepping stone, his hand firmly held by mine, while I in turn was anchored by the group. Neil advanced to his next stepping stone, and then his next, while I followed him and the rest of the group shifted and stretched to hold anchorage.

Now Neil seemed pleased with his position. He bent down close to the rushing water in the center of the spring. He had his eye on a certain level rock that was recessed a bit from the rushing water and could serve as a kind of sheltered offering place or shrine. I sensed the emotion welling up in Neil again. His whole energy state took on a kind of solemn shamanic focus. I could tell he wanted to position the crystal *just right.* He reached toward the sheltered rock and poised the crystal just above it. He paused and checked his instincts. He drew a little closer. He nearly placed the crystal, then paused again, double checked his instincts, drew even closer, decided everything was perfect, and gently placed the crystal on the rock. In that instant I witnessed one of the most remarkable energy events I have ever seen, on Mt. Shasta or anywhere else. Neil, meanwhile, had apparently decided that perhaps his placement of the crystal wasn't quite right after all. He was reaching to retrieve the crystal, but *the crystal wasn't there anymore.* So he rose, and we "retracted" the human bridge back to the gathering spot on the bank. "It's very strange!" said Neil. "I had just put the crystal down on the rock for a second, but then I couldn't find it anymore. I don't know what happened to it."

It was time for me to share what I had witnessed. In the split second when Neil released the crystal to the mountain, the crystal was swept right out of the physical dimension and ushered into the etheric dimension of pure light within the mountain where a host of the ascended masters and beloved spirit guides who help to guide our human lives had gathered to receive the crystal—and, really, *to receive us.*

"We put ourselves into that crystal for good reason, it seems," I said. "To the masters and guides the crystal was like a photo album, from us to them."

My own emotion swelled as I got to the most important part: *"They received us with so much love.*

"It's like they opened their collective presence to receive us as honored guests. They were thrilled to have us there with them. We are with them even now. They want us to know that we belong, we fit, that each and every one of us carries within us the same divine light that they have learned to purely live in.

"They want us to know how much we all make a difference in every single moment when we shine our light and unfold our love. We are destined, unless we block it, to live purely in divine light and love, as they do. They want us to know that nothing is worth blocking this higher destiny, nothing at all. They already see us in our destined purity and brilliance. They see us as vessels of the same divine light and love that they carry. They see us from the truth of equality. Equality *is* the higher truth, and the masters see us not so much as aspirants toiling on the path, but as awakening masters in our own right. And they see us as free, completely free to have our awakening and have our mastery."

My words trailed off. The energy of the experience carried us deeper. It felt very timeless, to be recognized in this way, to be recognized as who we really are.

I am certain that this experience has transformed the awareness of every one of us. I am certain that this recognition still lives within us. We are not just aspirants on the path, we are awakening masters in our own right.

✧   ✧   ✧

Envision your freedom. You are free to be who you really are. You have learned to let go of conditional identity. You have learned to live without errant identification instincts or misguided identification phenomena. You have learned to discern and to leave behind you even the aspirant instinct that seeks out more "spiritual" conditional identities or special roles.

You have radically allowed that you are, simply, free.

Everything feels different now. Your very presence feels different now. It is more subtle and fluid. It has less definition, perhaps, than you had been accustomed to. You are experiencing a presence and a consciousness, now, that lies beneath the ever-changing outer conditions of your life and beneath the ever-changing, conditional responses to your life that used to be so familiar to you.

You are experiencing *a presence that holds the consciousness for life itself, for the real thing, the essence, the foundation, the enduring, unlimited, unconditional sacred aliveness itself.*

You relax into this.

You relax into soul presence.

Soul Presence

Soul is all about presence. Soul *is* presence.

Soul is the sacred presence that abides through all time—soul is the enduring part of us that is, distinctly, not mortal.

Soul is true identity, the true self that comes shining through when we transcend the conditional self.

Soul, we discover, is the real presence that has been here all along, doing the incarnating. It's not like some other presence, some limited, egoic self has been here all along doing the incarnating. We saw this very clearly in the previous chapter. Limited, egoic selves arise *from* the incarnation experience, from the pressures and stresses of incarnate life and from our conditional responses to life stress. Because limited egoic selves arise *from* the incarnation experience, they cannot be the true presence that is in fact doing the incarnating. We have learned how ego may try to blur or even to exile our true soul presence by investing in separation dramas. To whatever degree the belief in separation gets foregrounded in our awareness, soul is kept in the background, held in check. It's no wonder then, that our soul presence, as we awaken into it, may seem subtler and less defined than what we are used to. *It is.* Our soul identity is so subtle that it understands not separation, but oneness.

While separation dramas may hinder the soul's ability to "ensoul" our human adventure fully, yet the soul always abides, and does its best to keep the incarnation experience on track, holding it all together, waiting for its chances to incarnate more, bidding for what evolution it can. For our soul is what does the evolving. As we saw in Chapter 15, ego or false presence cannot evolve. But soul evolves by incarnating its divine potentials into the human arena and letting them express and grow. Soul evolves through a spiraling journey, as we traced it in Chapter 5, of learning to own its innocence and grace, its divinely endowed, most natural state of soul freedom and sacred aliveness, with ever greater maturity, command, and conscious wholeness. Soul evolves by awakening its divinity, awakening the kingdom of Spirit within, and then, as we saw in Chapter 9, having *reflections* of its divinity added. Soul is the true presence and, distinctly, the only presence that can have "all else added unto it."

Soul understands what the spirit guides and masters imparted to the Mt. Shasta group that day by the waterfall.

Soul understands *coming unconditionally alive.*

Soul Is a Spark of the Infinite Spirit

Soul understands coming unconditionally alive because it is a spark of the infinite Spirit. That's what soul is, a spark or individuated life-stream or consciousness-stream, that springs from the unconditional aliveness of the infinite divine Source and expresses the aliveness of the infinite divine Source, *as* the Source in individuated form. That is why soul is sometimes called the "child of God." It is the *atman,* or individuated spark of the cosmic Oneness known in India as Brahman. It is the consciousness that holds the space for miracles, for the miracle of Formlessness expressing into form. It is the beloved "heir to the kingdom" who is endowed with all that Spirit is—love, light, creative power, joy, peace, wisdom, beauty, pure unconditional aliveness, infinite good, sacred wholeness. Soul is the adventurer consciousness that takes these attributes of Spirit and seeks to express them in the manifest worlds of time and form. It is the journeyer through time, lifetime after lifetime, with one foot in time and the other foot in the timeless.

Soul is the pilgrim consciousness that sets out to learn all about how the universe works so that it can master the workings of God's universe and return to the Source, to the Godhead of cosmic intelligence, in conscious mastery. That's why the spirit guides that day by the waterfall on Mt. Shasta recognized us as awakening masters.

Descriptions of soul such as these abound in metaphysical literature, both classical and contemporary, and may be familiar to most readers. The real sense of these descriptions is articulated quite nicely in a contemporary expression that has become deservedly popular—

We are spiritual beings having a human adventure.

In other words, we often think of ourselves as human beings trying to figure out how to be more spiritual, but the opposite is true. We are spiritual beings, and what we are trying to figure out is how to be human. That's a pretty good description of what it means to be an incarnate soul.

While all of these descriptions are very helpful, I personally find most useful the simple description of soul that has evolved for me over time—

Soul is the sacred inner essence of us
that abides in divine love,
is commissioned in divine love,
and, true to its mission, simply will not stop loving.

For me, this is how to identify and to know when we're in touch with soul presence. We're in touch with soul presence when we're in touch with the part of us that won't stop loving. As I shared earlier, in Chapter 8, this working definition cuts to the chase and provides a practical and incisive handle for *experiencing* soul presence and for *being* soul presence. Soul presence inheres in pure love. We find soul presence in the mission to stay true to love.

Soul Perspective: Peace and Passion

As I've learned to stay true to love and to surrender into this sacred soul presence within me that won't stop loving, I have come to
see everything going on in my life as much like the shifting currents
of a wide, expansive river, a river with two opposite shores. These
shores are—

   ✧ Soul peace; and
   ✧ Soul passion.

From the shore of soul peace, what I see is—

   ✧ Nothing matters, but that I am present to it in
     unconditional love.

From the shore of soul passion, what I see is—

   ✧ Everything matters, as I am present to it in
     unconditional love.

From either shore, awakening soul consciousness knows how to stay
present, and how to stay present *in love*. Soul has a real genius for
doing this. It is this soul genius for staying fully present, in love,
that drives the whole adventure of coming unconditionally alive, for
pure divine love is the deepest essence of Spirit, and coming alive all
the way, coming alive in Spirit, *must* be founded on unconditional
loving presence.

   Let's explore how it works. It seems simple, but there is nothing
simplistic or unsophisticated about it.

It starts with pure presence. Pure presence is pure consciousness. This pure presence/pure consciousness needs to find a way to entertain the ever-changing experience of human life, the shifting currents of the river, without being distorted, shaken, or even seemingly lost in the flux of it all. This pure presence needs to find a way to embrace the river of life from the broadest and most stable perspective it possibly can. Pure presence needs to find the one common element that, beneath the flux of our lives, ultimately *matters.*

Otherwise, we tend to get caught up in the currents of the river on their own level, and then our whole sense of what matters tends to become jumbled, uncertain, distressingly conditional. At times like this our awareness may flit from one conditioned mind perspective to another and then slip, often, into staking our happiness on how well we're managing the conditions. But if we can leverage ourselves back into a broader perspective, then we can feel balanced and free again. Then we can be fully present and fully conscious, but without the drama. We stay free.

It takes a certain *leveraging* skill to do this. We get our leverage from the soul, from the genius of the soul. For the soul knows how to embrace life from its opposite shores, from the shore of soul peace and from the shore of soul passion. And the soul knows how to uphold the common element, the one thing that ultimately matters. The soul knows, at the very core of its genius, that *Nothing matters, but that we are present to it in our unconditional love, and then—but only then, as we are present in our unconditional love—then everything matters.*

Leveraging

I once saw a bumper sticker that read, "I'm already talking to my-self, now I just need to say the right things." That's a good one. We need little reminders sometimes. We need to find ways to keep discerning what matters. I often find myself, in soulful little moments, reminding myself of the axiom of soul peace, "Nothing matters, but that I am present to it in unconditional love." Often the short form—simply, "nothing matters"—feels most effective, most leveraging. It's like clicking the *Refresh* button on the screen of my mind. Sometimes I almost feel like we should have a variant on the *Refresh* button, a *Nothing Matters* button. Reminding myself that nothing matters helps free my awareness to let go, expand, and get back in touch with the inner peace of soul presence. If I'm adept I can really move into the profound inner fullness of this, into the preeminent fullness of the only presence that is enduring and real. I can relax into the full-ness that transcends all needs and all human drama. The shore of soul peace is a consummately restorative shore. This is the fullness of our pure beingness. It's a lovely experience to just rest in this.

Equally agreeable is what happens next. The state of pure being al-ways swells, from within its own fullness, into new waves of activity. This is true on a cosmic scale, and on a personal scale as well.[7] It is simply remarkable to be resting deeply in pure beingness, when sud-denly the exquisite restfulness swells. At these moments I feel like a timeless cycle is replaying, with utter freshness, in my conscious-ness. I am the witness. I am holding the space in consciousness. I am not doing anything at all to cause this stirring, yet the state of pure beingness is stirring and swelling into new waves. I feel these waves moving in my awareness. They are unmistakable. They are the unique

---

7 See pages 47, 66, 67, and 84–85.

and unmistakable essence of Spirit on the move—they are waves of divine love.

Spirit is on the move, doing what Spirit does. Without my having done a single thing to make this happen, the living Spirit at the core of my beingness is rising and expressing in fresh waves of love. I directly sense how this cycle that is replaying in my awareness is a timeless one. I sense that I am privy to the same ineffable renewal that every saint and bodhisattva must surely live in.

As the waves of new love rise, they refresh love's inherent, ineffable promise to illumine and transform everything that love interacts with. Suddenly, *everything* matters. In the presence of love everything matters totally, it couldn't matter more! My role becomes more than just to be present and open for Spirit's irrepressible love to flow through me, my role becomes—

To make Spirit's love <u>personal</u>
here in the world of time and space
and real events and real people.

This makes all the difference. This means everything as far as the soul's role in the grand scheme of things is concerned. The fresh passion of this awareness frees me to connect once again, in heightened appreciation and spontaneous blessing, with the dance of co-creation that is my personal life. I renew the dance and I bless the dance as I come present to it, once again, in unconditional love. I have become the focal point where the unbounded, universal love of the infinite Spirit becomes *personal.*

This is soul perspective.

Soul Perspective, Being, and Becoming

Soul perspective keeps our inner lives on course. The more we swing in the soul rhythm of peace and passion the more we learn to center in the essence, in the unconditional love. It becomes exquisitely freeing to just center in the love and let the details of life flow along like a river. Soon we find that we can observe the river of our lives from *both* shores at the *same time.* This holds us in a delicious creative tension—nothing matters yet everything matters—that refines our consciousness to new depths of subtlety, transcendence, and conscious union with the universal sacred aliveness.

In such moments we may even tune in to the cosmic rhythm of Being and Becoming. We may glimpse, that is, the sacred cosmic process in which the pure Beingness of Spirit rises into new forms and new life in the universe.

At moments like this we are glimpsing the opposite shores—to keep the river analogy—of the river of *cosmic* life. For Being and Becoming are the most fundamental pair of opposites in cosmic life.

It's a startlingly beautiful experience to see how our own personal rhythm of soul peace and soul passion is recapitulating and *making personal* this deepest rhythm of cosmic life.

✧ Our experience of soul peace is how we make the pure, transcendent Being *personal.*

✧ Our experience of soul passion is how we make the sacred act of cosmic Becoming *personal.*

What a role we play. As we awaken our soul consciousness and learn to swing in the rhythm of soul peace and soul passion, we are recapitulating the deepest rhythm of cosmic life and making the creative tempo of cosmic life come alive on a personal level. It's like our own personal re-enactment of the power and the intelligence and the creative beat of the universe.

To the awakened soul, it becomes more than a re-enactment. It becomes an ongoing dharma of consecrating life and re-consecrating life. With each soul-conscious moment, as we embrace the opposite shores of the river of life, drawing powerfully from our fundamental, true peace, drawing powerfully from our our fundamental, true passion, and staying free, each changing moment, to abide in pure divine love, we are consecrating life and celebrating life and forever re-consecrating, like gracious stewards, the deepest creative rhythm of life.

Soul Perspective and Happiness

I find that when I can live consciously in the rhythms of the soul, this is when all the qualities of the living Spirit come most alive in my awareness, not just the peace and the passion, not just the essence love, but *all* the qualities of Spirit. This is when I can most feel the timelessness of Spirit. This is when I can most feel the vastness of Spirit. This is when I can most clearly experience the exquisite light frequencies of the Infinite. This is when I can feel the healing energies of Spirit, and the actual energy blessings of Spirit, distinct currents of energy, flowing into me. This is when my awareness can vibrate most naturally in respect, and compassion, and tenderness, and kindness.

This is when I can simply *be* the pure, unconditional *loving presence* that is Spirit.

It's at times like this that the living wisdom of Spirit comes alive and starts to illumine my life like never before. This is when all the points of spiritual wisdom can really *work* for me, elegantly, and reliably. Here is an example that is especially germane. I have always loved the point from *A Course in Miracles* that suggests that we can always choose to be genuinely happy simply because any and all supposed reasons for not being happy are, to the expanded mind, not really relevant to true happiness anyhow. I find in this point a lovely and cogent way to work with the distinction between happiness and mere okayness (a distinction that we developed in the previous chapter). It is so humbling, sometimes, to see how easily the mind can get confused about happiness when the inner terrain of the mind becomes contracted and slips out of soul perspective. I have needed to track this one carefully, first-hand—

✧ The triggering of okayness issues becomes, to the contracted and imbalanced mind, a *reason for not being "happy."*

✧ Conversely, the resolution of okayness issues becomes, to the contracted and imbalanced mind, a *reason for being "happy."*

What's true, of course, is that this form of being "happy" or not being "happy" is so utterly conditional that it is not about real happiness at all. Real happiness is not condition-sensitive. But it takes the soul perspective to realize this. Soul perspective can, effectively, *pre-empt* the conditional approach to happiness. That's another one of the qualities of Spirit—Spirit is pre-emptive.

Real happiness quickens and grows with astonishing freshness and lucidity when we're in soul perspective, when we are so centered in our unconditional love that we know and appreciate, with every pulse of our being, that *nothing else matters but the love.* In this state nothing could possibly "matter" in the sense of taking us out of our happiness. The happiness is unconditional. It's an exquisite and indescribable feeling, to feel this much freedom. This is the freedom of the soul to live in unconditional joy. We can taste this freedom in times of reflection and meditation. And we *live* this freedom when we live in unconditional love. It is not possible to live in unconditional love and not be happy. In fact this is why we are, after all, commissioned in love. Spirit wants us to be happy, and Spirit knows that *it is not possible to live in unconditional love and not be happy.* To see ourselves as divinely commissioned in love is not a simplistic or unsophisticated perspective—it is simply seeing ourselves as on the path to life's most natural outcome, on the path, that is, to the fulfillment that Spirit has had in mind for us from the beginning.

Love, Synergy, Mysticism and Miracles

Soul perspective works because of the synergy. Peace feeds passion, while passion feeds peace. The more we grow in peace, the more we grow in passion. The more we learn that nothing matters, the more we learn that everything matters. This synergy needs to work both ways, else our passionate embrace of life would become imbalanced. And so the more we embrace life in passion, the more we are called back to peace. The more we learn that everything matters, the more we are called back to learning that nothing matters.

Most of all, as we swing in this rhythm, we learn to live in its essence, in the sacred synergistic element that holds it all together, the pure divine love, the *sine qua non,* without which nothing matters but in which everything matters totally, in which everything starts to matter quite *mystically.*

We become mystical: We become sensitized to how everything in our world can open up to reveal so much more than the apparent and the ordinary. We become passionate to participate in this. We seek out the mystical thresholds in our consciousness and in our world. We see how—

Mystical thresholds occur
as our world and our consciousness
come together in love.

We see how the mystical dimension of conscious living is all about the love, the intimacy, the *romance* that is ripening between our consciousness and our world.

We become a mystic and a lover as we romance this world of ours. Our world comes alive with profound and even miraculous new possibilities in the presence of our love. We are learning what our love is capable of.

Divine love really is unconditional.
And unconditonal love really is unstoppable.
This is why, as awakening souls commissioned in this love,
we really won't stop loving.

Our mystical soul passion rises to fresh heights as it glimpses the new horizon of what is possible with this love—

Since this love within us won't stop,
it will not stop short of—miracles.

Miracles, we discover, are the upshot of unconditional love and the outcome of unconditional love. Miracles are the emergence of potent, life-changing new possibilities, previously unforeseeable, from the synergistic action of divine love in our world.

✧　　　✧　　　✧

Envision your freedom. You have become a conscious soul, a mystic and a lover. You live in unconditional joy. Unconditional joy lives in you. You live in love. Love lives in you. The love keeps you whole, balanced and free. The love keeps you holding the space for miracles.

In your freedom you find it very easy and gracious to keep practicing soul presence. You know how to simply *be* this presence, the presence that hosts and incarnates, with conscious passion and conscious peace, the universal sacred aliveness. You hold the space for the universal sacred aliveness to live in you. You hold the space for sacred aliveness to quicken in your world and to threshold into your impassioned mystical awareness. You are learning how, when your awareness is tuned, everything reveals the sacred.

You are beckoning this with all your love.

You are learning that the key is to deeply, deeply tune your awareness. So you are beckoning the synergistic power of love into your inner world, into the inner terrain of your mind. You want your miracle here.

Your mind has grown quite fit. It knows how to allow life and not resist life. Life keeps happening, and you have learned to allow all the parts of life, including the parts that make your mind contract. You know how to let your mind navigate the condition-sensitive parts of being human. Besides, you know that nothing ultimately matters, no matter how contractive, but that you are present to it in your love. Even great challenge or great stress matter to you *as* you are present to the challenge, *as* you are present to the stress, *in* your love. You have learned that staying present in your love is really the same thing as staying present as who you really are. You are very clear about who you are—a divine soul commissioned in love, a conscious divine soul who won't stop loving. So you simply love the contractive phases of your mind. You bless the stress. There's nothing else to do! You stay true to love. The notion of separating yourself from this love does not occur to you. Separation does not occur to you. Fear and anxiety, the products of separation, do not occur to you either— or, if they do, however fleetingly, you see them as unfounded. For you know, in the constancy of your love, that life subsists in sacred wholeness and that separation is an illusion. You find that you can stay true to love. You find that you can love your conditioned mind, you can love the contraction, compassionately, compassionately, you can love any fear or anxiety or judgment or any of the other layered emotions that may spring from separation feelings. You are still very human—but *you can love it all.*

Now your mystical instincts are really inspired. You want to see what happens as you perfect this way of being so compassionate, so unconditionally loving, with the inner life of your mind.

At first you may hardly realize how deeply the inner life of your mind is transforming. The transformation unfolds so naturally.

In time the depth of the transformation becomes evident. In time, you realize that your mind has become completely free.

Yes, your mind still navigates your experience of being human. Your mind still contracts as appropriate to deal with all the conditions that have a bearing on your human okayness. To adapt an old expression, you chop wood when you need wood and you carry water when you need water, and you draw your mind into all the focus that is needed to perform these tasks, and all tasks. *But now your mind is free.* Now your mind is profoundly free. No matter how much your mind may contract as outer circumstances warrant, your mind is *not* contracted. Miraculous as it may seem, your mind is permanently and profoundly expanded, even in the midst of the most focused tasks. The freedom of this is ineffably satisfying. Your mind embraces and unifies, simultaneously and without conflict, the condition-sensitive ranges of itself along with the frequency ranges that vibrate in pure, unconditional happiness and universal sacred aliveness. To you it is all One Mind. To you it is all sacred. Your personal mind has bonded, consciously, to the life of the One Mind.

You relax into this.

You relax into conscious soul freedom.

Chapter 17

Co-Creating a Sacred World

Over time, the evidence of unconditional love grows stronger in our shared world.

How we are choosing to be present, in every moment of time, imprints this quantum world we live in and hence "votes," in effect, for the kind of world we want to have.

We could think of this voting as a kind of worldwide review process, much like an election or a referendum. As we suggested in Chapter 12—

⋄ The old paradigm of life in separation, conflict, and fear is being challenged and brought under review; while

⋄ The new paradigm of life in conscious soul freedom, unconditional joy, wholeness, and universal sacred aliveness is bidding for ascendancy.

As we said earlier, the "ballot" in this election is nothing less than the quantum world in which we live, the very fabric or plasma of responsive energy that is always imprinted and directed by what goes on in the consciousness of every single one of us, every single moment.

✧ Every time any one of us chooses to be present as a conscious soul, as a loving, trusting, conscious co-participant in the universal sacred aliveness, the worldwide "ballot" registers a vote for the new paradigm.

✧ Every time any one of us chooses to withhold or cloak our true presence in old patterns of separation and fear, the world sags with yet another vote for the old paradigm.

All voting trends are continuously tallied and reckoned—and then directly fed back into our consciousness as the actual state of the world we live in.

This way, no one need wonder about how our consciousness habits are affecting the world.

And no one need wonder but that this election is for real.

Accountability

We live in a time of unparalleled opportunity to transform the state of the world. We live, as well, in a time of unparalleled responsibility. Our true dharma, our sacred duty to fully and maturely incarnate the living Spirit in all its creative power and infinite good, has never been more vitally important than it is now. Will we draw our presence from the living Spirit, will we learn to source our lives, consciously, from our divine Source? Will we learn to bless our world and to bless our lives in the world, to see it all as Spirit sees it, as a living ocean of divine potentials, each wave on the ocean lovingly supported to evolve to its highest expression of the pure creative light and wisdom and power and peace and love and wholeness and exquisite joy of its infinite Source?

Or will we settle for life on the planet as humanity has known it up until now? The choice is ours.

In many ways, the times we live in are extraordinarily inspiring. More and more people are learning to wake up and, as we are look around, we can see the light of the Higher Presence growing brighter in each other's eyes. We can hear the power and wisdom of our Higher Presence, if we are listening, growing more resonant in each other's voices. We are learning to feel the sacredness, the sacred aliveness of the Higher Presence, pulsing stronger in our individual presence. And we can see each other standing more fully in our truth and owning more genuinely our soul freedom to live consciously from the Source. We sense that humanity is evolving toward a new and higher way to be, a new paradigm for how to live, a higher destiny. Our sense of a higher destiny seems confirmed by many of the spiritual teachings and traditions, from Buddhist to Mayan to new physics to New Thought, that inform our sense of these evolving times. And we feel the Sacred Feminine on the move, rising in the awakening consciousness of our times to champion the values of nurturance, respect, tenderness, interconnectedness, and accountability so desperately needed, in these pivotal times, to balance and bless human activity and to ensure that the world we co-create is one in which the divine potentials of life are not subverted or suppressed but are truly served and honored. This is the Divine Mother's vision and the Divine Mother's passion. Like a mother raises her child to reach its full potential, Divine Mother is doing all She can to "raise the universe" and raise the awareness of the human family into conscious co-creation of a sacred world.

Spiritual Grown-Ups

These are times for growing up spiritually. We are called to become very mature, very fit, very conscious, incarnating the Higher

Presence as impeccably as we can, taking our moment-to-moment presence to the highest level of dharma, making our conscious presence a spiritual practice, one that we practice continuously, not just when we're feeling inspired.

For all we know, the cosmic referendum will be closed soon.

For all we know, the voting will end at a moment of great uncertainty and turbulence, at a moment, perhaps, when the desperate efforts of old paradigm forces are at their most critical. Will we be true to love and wholeness in that moment? Or will the turbulence of the moment throw us once again into separation and trigger in us precisely the energies of anger, judgment and fear that have driven the old paradigm for so long? Will we find ourselves staying present enough to the situation to be able to source true wisdom and strength? Will we be able to stay present enough in our love and wholeness to attract to any crisis the blessing it so critically needs in order to resolve and heal?

Every moment matters. The worldwide "ballot" is tallying our votes even now. This is why the key to spiritual maturity is learning to be fully present and to stay fully present. Spiritual "grown-ups" learn how to stay fully present in *all* circumstances.

"How Do We Know When We're Being Fully Present?"

Over time, the workshops I lead seem to have coalesced and refined. They have moved from exploring a great many aspects of the spiritual journey, each aspect valuable in its own way, to exploring this very simple, very essential spiritual practice—the practice of being fully *present*.

I will never forget a particular workshop in Kalamazoo, Michigan when, as the group awareness refined and coalesced into this simple realization that the whole journey of spiritual awakening comes down to this, to being fully and consciously present as embodiments of the living Spirit, one of the group participants asked—

"But how do we know when we're being fully present?"

My natural approach to leading workshops is to work without a plan, to stay spontaneously present to the play and interplay of living wisdom within the group awareness. This way, leading groups keeps me practicing the essential point of staying present. I tend to not have standard answers to questions that may arise, and so I let each question threshold the group awareness into next stages of inquiry and awakening, in the moment. Each moment is a unique window, a portal into the activity of the Higher Presence and into the exquisite play of wisdom that is the life of the Higher Mind.

As I tuned to the energy of this group, in this moment, I saw that the learning threshold for the group was all about unconditional love. I took my cues. "We can know that we are being fully present," I began, "when we are fully in our love." The room stirred with resonance. "When we're present in unconditional love, that's when we're present all the way."

"Presencing Love"

"It's about *'presencing'* love," I continued, "and 'presencing' love so impeccably well that *there's enough for everyone and everything,* equally and unconditionally. That's the key—whatever we 'source' or 'presence' purely from Spirit expresses in us unconditionally. As we've said about love many times, if we're not loving everyone and everything, we're not really loving anyone, or anything. Love doesn't pick and choose."

Heads nodded, hearts opened. The play of living wisdom was growing very palpable in the group energy state. We were being upgraded, we were being carried, as a group, into a heightened state of spiritual presence that was founded in unconditional love and centered in unconditional love. We discussed it a bit longer, we tried to share in words how it felt—even as the energy of it all was carrying us beyond verbal sharing and into a time of giving ourselves over to what unconditional love is really about. We were feeling how unconditional love goes way beyond words, how *unconditional love seeks to share itself*, purely, directly, completely.

I facilitated. It was time for us to stand. I reminded the group that it is not up to us to generate the love. Spirit does that part. Spirit sources and supplies an unlimited flow of love. Our job is to be present as open vessels allowing this pure love to live and express in us. This is how we make spiritual love *personal.* And making spiritual love personal is what impassions the soul.

It was time to leave behind our notes and our personal thoughts and to come fully present to each other, one on one, one at a time, fully present to each one, eye to eye, heart to heart, without words, fully present in our love, gifting each person with our love, receiving each person in their love, feeling the oneness, the one love, the one, unconditional love that unites us in one presence, one universal Presence, One Spirit.

Some individuals in the group were more ready for this experience than others. That's okay, that tends to be true in nearly every group. But whenever a spiritually potent energy is spreading in a group, the energy will carry even those who seem less fully tuned to its gifts. That's the power of group dynamics in spiritual workshop settings, where the natural synergies between individual and group are given free reign. That day in Kalamazoo, some individuals had never before been involved in a spiritual workshop like this, some individuals had come to this workshop knowing no one else or nearly no one else in the group, some individuals had never allowed themselves to come fully present to *any* one, in *any* setting—and yet all of us were swept up in the synergistic power of shared presence, of many hearts in one love, many human hearts presencing one divine love. The sharing lasted for the better part of an hour and featured many a soulful, glowing smile and not a few tears of gratitude and release.

Birthing the Future

I believe that we glimpsed the future that day. I believe that we glimpsed the higher destiny, the new paradigm for humanity. The particular words we use to describe this state, such as "destiny" or "new paradigm" or any other words, don't really matter—it is a very real energy state that *already exists.*

It already exists in the "space," if you will, of our probable future. And it is seeking birth. As such, it is already real enough to catch glimpses of.

I believe that we glimpse our higher future whenever we come together and bond in unconditional love—even as few as "two or more" individuals, as the old expression goes. Each time we do this, our little microcosm of shared presence becomes a window into the macrocosm of greater possibilities. We glimpse a new and higher turn on the evolutionary spiral, a time when every one of us can finally be recognized and embraced as who we really are—sons and daughters of the infinite living Spirit, consciously awakening souls, each one of us uniquely worthy, every one of us expressing and enshrining the divine potentials of our common Source with unique genius, beauty and grace, all of us coming alive together in a powerful synergistic force-field of transformation and new possibilities. These microcosmic events, each on its own scale, are drawing the human family as a whole closer and closer to the "big event," to the authentic, real birthing of the new and higher paradigm into our shared world.

"Heaven on Earth"

In some visionary perspectives this probable future might be referred to as *heaven,* and its birthing into our realm of real experience might be referred to as *bringing heaven on earth.* Will the new paradigm fulfill the age-old dream of heaven on earth? We don't know. No one can say for certain what the new paradigm will really be like. No teacher, no teaching or visionary source, no matter how illumined, can say for certain what the new paradigm will be like—simply because the power of *synergy* is deeply involved here.

Synergy

In the workings of synergy, when individual elements, such as awakening individuals, are brought together in harmony with each other to form a new whole—

✧ The whole that emerges is more than the sum of the parts that have come together to form the whole; and

✧ The true nature and behavior of such a synergistic whole cannot be known from knowing the nature and behavior of the parts.

We may know the individual elements very well, we may know how it feels as individuals to practice impeccable spiritual presence and unconditional love, we may even know how it feels to connect with other individuals on that level, but when a whole society or a whole population such as the human family itself catches on and is swept into the oneness, into the shared state of impeccable spiritual presence and unconditional love, the synergistic whole that emerges is simply beyond our present ability to grasp.

All that we can say for certain is that the new paradigm will be just that, a *new paradigm.* It will be a *whole new way of being alive together.*

This is, in all likelihood, very good news. This suggests that we can't even imagine how profoundly fulfilling the new paradigm is likely to be. More than we can imagine, the higher destiny that awaits us is likely to satisfy our heart's innermost desire for fulfillment.

We are in the realm of miracles here, a realm of unimaginable, unforeseeable breakthroughs into greater and greater good. Miracles occur naturally when the synergy is right. And—

We get the synergy right
when we bring in the element of Spirit
and get our relationship with Spirit right.

Then anything is possible. With Spirit all things become possible and our highest good becomes probable.

Getting Our Relationship with Spirit Right

At several stages of this book we have explored the idea that when we seek first the kingdom of the living Spirit, the kingdom of heaven, then all else can be added. We have come to understand, in Chapter 6, that "seek first" must be taken to mean *seek unconditionally,* that, in other words, the teaching works, our lives are blessed, renewed and evolved, when we seek Spirit *for the sake of Spirit, not for the sake of what we can get out of it.* It is when we are seeking Spirit for the sake of Spirit that we can come alive *in Spirit.* We can let go of our conditional awareness enough to come alive, unconditionally, in the universal sacred aliveness that is Spirit. Then we are truly open to receive our good. In chapter 9 we came to understand that there is really only one way for greater good to come to us, there is only one thing that can really be added to the life of Spirit in us, and that is the *reflections,* reflections of the ineffable sacred aliveness that is living and evolving in us, as us. These reflections give us a chance to see yet more clearly, in the proving ground of real human experience, the utter divinity of who we really are. We have come to understand that, ultimately, it's all about presencing the greatest gift of Spirit, presencing pure divine love.

> *When we are letting pure divine love live in us, as us,*
> *<u>then</u> all else can be added to us.*

Then we've got our relationship with Spirit right and *then* the infinite potentials of Spirit can swell into new expression as the power of synergy brings forth "miraculous" or previously unforeseeable breakthroughs into greater and greater good.

Taking It to the Next Level

Now let us take this understanding to a collective level. The vision is simple:

> *When we are letting divine love live in us, as us, <u>collectively</u>,*
> *then all else can be added to us, <u>collectively</u>.*

Then we can have a sacred world.

Impeccable Means Impeccable

Will this sacred world bring heaven on earth? We suspect it will, although, again, we don't know for sure, we cannot really know until we get there.

And we have quite a ways to go before we get there.

Until the new paradigm truly dawns, we are in process. In fact, the more we sense the dawn of the new paradigm drawing near, the more we are likely to encounter everything within us that would block or frustrate our ability to really have a sacred world. We need to meet these inner blocks and issues with radical trust, with spiritual fitness, learning to transcend judgment, anger, fear and weakness and to stay true to love—learning, in effect, to *keep voting for the new paradigm, every moment,* since every single vote affects the outcome. As the new paradigm draws nearer and nearer, our ability to really have a sacred world will be founded in this same spiritual fitness, this same ability to practice impeccable spiritual presence and unconditional love.

It always comes down to fitness.

Our fitness gives the universe its cues about what we are ready for.

Blending Heaven and Earth

Energetically, our fitness develops in our system of chakras and tunes our chakras to function powerfully. It's our chakras that ply our whole energetic relationship with the living universe. All of the chakras are involved in this ongoing relationship, while three of them—

- ✧ The crown chakra,
- ✧ The base chakra, and
- ✧ The heart chakra

are especially involved. As we saw in Chapters 14 and 12, the crown plies our relationship with the higher planes or the "heavens," while the base chakra plies our relationship with the earth plane. And we need both, both the heavens and the earth are equally important parts of this multi-dimensional living universe. We receive energy blessings and energy upgrades from the higher planes at the crown, while the base chakra, in turn, receives energy blessings and energy upgrades from the earth.

What about the heart chakra?

The heart plays a very special role. The heart is uniquely suited to harmonize, to blend the energies of the heavens with the energies of the earth. The heart is where our "rainbow" role in the universe is served,[8] where our uniquely human station in this grand cosmos of living energies finds fulfillment.

It is in our hearts
where the real meeting of heaven and earth
is meant to take place.

When we threshold into this, into discovering that our own heart is precisely where the energies of heaven and earth are destined to meet, blend, and synergize—this one event sends evolutionary ripples through all levels of our being, and into the universe itself.

The Evolving Universe

The universe itself is directly affected. The universe itself is seeking its next stages of evolution, just as all other manifest forms are. The universe is seeking to bring forth new and ever more potent synergies, new expressions of sacred wholeness, higher and higher

---

8 In Native American lore, one of the original words for "human" means, literally, *rainbow*. (See page 158.)

configurations of the infinite divine potentials of life. What this evolving universe seeks most of all, what this evolving universe yearns for,
is *to heal all separation, to harmonize the dimensions, to bring the
blessings of the higher planes flooding into our earthly world.*

And the universe has chosen us as its focal point, its "cutting
edge" of evolution, its co-creator.

We co-create with the universe and co-evolve with the universe
when we bring our heart chakra powerfully into the equation.

There is an old saying in Sufism that "Neither the heavens nor
the earth can contain Me [the One Spirit], but the heart of my beloved
faithful servant can." The heart can hold what neither the heavens
nor the earth can contain—that is a remarkable statement! Similar
descriptions of the extraordinary power of the human heart occur in
all of the mystical teachings. The ascended master Saint Germain, for
example, has always pointedly affirmed that as our evolution accel-
erates and our energy state becomes more and more charged and
invigorated with spiritually galvanizing energies, *our heart can hold
it all, our heart can integrate it all.* And the Sacred Feminine, the
cosmic Mother, holds special favor for precisely this, the evolution
of our hearts. In Her tireless work to raise the universe to its highest evolutionary potential, the Sacred Feminine finds Her greatest
pleasure in coaxing our hearts to come fully alive, for She knows that
the divine energy of *universal compassion, once it is fully awakened
in the human heart, will powerfully assist the universe in its evolutionary imperative to heal all separation, to harmonize the dimensions, and to bring the blessings of the higher planes flooding into our
earthly world.*

Our very soul stirs when we begin to grasp the transformational
power and alchemy that lies deep in our hearts. Our soul knows that
when the power of the heart is fully awakened, our deepest soul wisdom will finally quicken and take ascendancy in our lives.

Our soul knows that this will make all the difference, this will redefine incarnate life as we know it—this will *fundamentally* shift the paradigm of incarnate life on our planet.

Cutting Edge

To awaken the heart into its higher potential, we must become a visionary and a lover. We must become a lover of miracles. We must become soulfully present and sensitized to the mystical thresholds opening up in the interface between our consciousness and our world. We must envision each present moment pressing and expressing into the realm of new evolutionary possibilities. We must become a lover of the astonishing power of this synergistic universe to birth new and higher configurations of the infinite divine potentials of life. We must be willing to live at the cutting edge of what is possible.

Energetically, we must open and tune our energy state so that our heart can be flushed with new aliveness and quickened into its co-creative role in the universe. When our intention for this is clear and impassioned, the simple expression *"I am here for the greater good of all"* works powerfully, like a catalyst or a seed mantra, I have found, to get the process started. When we affirm "I am here for the greater good of all,"

- ✧ Our base chakra is re-invigorated and our crown chakra is re-invigorated.[9]
- ✧ Our grounded presence *as an individual* is harmonized with our open, trusting presence *as a part of the universal whole.*

---

9 The effect is greatest, of course, when these chakras have become very accustomed to conscious use. To help these chakras become truly fit and accustomed to conscious use you may want to spend more time with the material on developing them, in Chapters 12 and 14.

✧ Most of all, our very way of being present begins to upgrade and to feel like what it is really meant to be—

In the greater scheme of things
our conscious presence is the cutting edge
where the evolving universe is seeking to heal separation
and to co-create new evolutionary potentials,
new synergies, even miracles.

Awakening the Heart

Give yourself to this now. Relax, take a few breaths, and start tuning in as you silently affirm, "I am here for the greater good of all." Let go of any personal thoughts and feelings that may have been holding your awareness in separation or tension. Just for now, let it be enough to know that you are here for the greater good of all. Let this way of being present pre-empt the tensions of the conditioned mind. Take a few more breaths.

Give yourself into the experience. You are opening into a greater good. You are here in the service of synergy, miracles, and new evolutionary potentials. Feel your base chakra activate as it grounds your presence on the earth plane. Feel your crown chakra quicken as it opens your presence to the workings of the higher planes. Let yourself be open and invigorated. You are an energy being. You live in a quantum energy universe. One unconditional sacred life-force interconnects all things and seeks to harmonize all things into a common, greater good. Feel the sacred aliveness of the earth flow into you at the base while the sacred aliveness of the higher planes flows into you at the crown. Let the multi-dimensional universe lift you now, and flush you with its exquisite sacred aliveness. Open to receive. Draw in energy. If you are tuned in to light frequencies, be sure to draw in cosmic gold light, as this is the best frequency for healing separation and restoring wholeness.

Now draw all these energies toward the center of your being, draw these energies to your heart chakra. *The heart can receive it all.* Let your heart open and receive the exquisite sacred aliveness of this living universe. Let your heart come powerfully alive. Keep drawing energy. Draw the energy blessings of the earth. Draw the energy blessings of the heavens. Draw them to your heart. *Your heart can integrate it all.* Your heart can harmonize and blend them to create something greater, to create something so potent that it transcends what either the heavens alone or the earth alone can contain. This moment is invaluable. Give yourself fully to it. You are taking your personal fitness to a profound new stage. As you blend the energies of heaven and earth in your heart, you are at the cutting edge of co-creation and co-evolution. You are in the realm of synergy. You are bringing forth a new expression of the infinite potentials of the universal life-force. You are bringing forth a new and unforeseeably powerful heart-space, a synergistic new state of heart awareness that is so mature, so fit, that it can command, with utter certainty, the deepest knowing of your soul—

There is nothing that is not sacred.
There is nothing that is not the One.
There is only the One,

the infinite living Spirit.
I am a part of the One,
a part of the sacred whole.
In this sacred Oneness I am free.
I am free to live in
unconditional sacred aliveness.
I am free to see as Spirit sees,
to bless as Spirit blesses,
and to love as Spirit loves,
compassionately, unconditionally.

Center in this. There is only the One. There is only the infinite living Spirit. As a part of the One, you are free to have your highest good unfold in unconditional sacred aliveness, and to have your highest good perfectly aligned to the greater good of all. Feel the certainty, the absolute, transcendent certainty. This knowing transcends all thought and reflection. This knowing is self-evident and self-sufficient. This knowing is absolutely certain. And your heart has achieved it.

Now your heart can own it.

Co-Creating a Sacred World

Now there is a new signal in the universe.

Now the cosmic sacred Oneness is growing strong in another conscious human heart.

Now the light of Oneness is spreading.

More and more hearts will awaken to the light of sacred Oneness. The light will spread and suffuse itself into our world.

Then the separation will truly heal. Then the paradigm of separation will finally yield. Then the dimensions will truly harmonize and the blessings of the spiritual planes will come flooding into our world.

✧   ✧   ✧

Then we can co-create a sacred world.

CDs by Mark Schoofs
Recorded live at workshops nationwide

Soul Freedom, Sacred Aliveness

Soul awakening and planetary transformation are advancing hand in hand in our times, building a cogent new paradigm for evolving humanity: we are sacred, multi-dimensional beings exploring transformational energies with a divine commission to co-create a sacred world. We are powerfully drawn to the conscious experience of the divine soul, the sacred, true Self within, and to live in conscious soul freedom. From here we can explore the transformational energy events, thresholds, and outcomes of the soul's journey to wholeness.

Opening to Mastery, Opening to Miracles

Immerse yourself in the freeing wisdom and power of the master within, that calls you to surrender your egoic agendas and to experience unconditional trust, pure happiness, renewal, and all the miraculous possibilities of life in spiritual freedom.

Soul-Conscious Living—
Passion, Peace, Perfected Love

Inviting the sacred, true Self within you to come fully alive in the sustaining rhythms of impeccable soulful presence.

Divine Mother—
Embracing the Sacred Feminine

The masculine principle of the infinite living Spirit *expresses* divinity while the feminine principle of Spirit *embodies* divinity and nurtures all manifest forms to their highest state of awakened divine potentials. Tune to the incomparable passion of the Sacred Feminine, and to Her exquisite healing love.

Grounding and Presence—
Incarnating the Spirit

Learn to ground deeply to the healing energies of the earth, to let go, and to live in freedom. Use conscious grounding to become powerfully centered in the abiding presence and peace of the living Spirit.

Awakening the Christ Consciousness

Christ consciousness is known by many names in all spiritual traditions, and beckons awakening souls to this mystical plane of self-mastery, perfected love, miracles, and joyous, egoless freedom.

Heightened Energy for the Body and Brain

Use these guided meditations and exercises, adapted from Tantra, to quicken the sacred aliveness in your nervous system, your chakras, and your brain.

To Order CDs
visit www.LightandLove.com/Books&CDs
all CDs $15 U.S.

CPSIA information can be obtained at www.ICGtesting.com
Printed in the USA
LVOW061248020612

284362LV00003B/4/P